WEATHERLY WAYPOINT GUIDE

Vol. 2:

Gulf of Georgia

Robert Hale

Weatherly Press
Bellevue, Washington

Your comments and corrections are invited. Please let us know if you find any significant errors in this publication. Also let us know if you find any waypoints that should be moved to more useful locations ("200 yards west of the buoy, not east"), or where you would want additional waypoints. In this way future editions can be changed and improved.

Write to:

Weatherly Press
Waypoint Guide
1803 132nd Ave. NE, Suite 4
Bellevue, WA 98005
Telephone (206) 881-5212

Changes, additions and corrections to all three Weatherly Waypoint Guide volumes will be posted on their own page at our web site www.waggonerguide.com.

Acknowledgments

Many people have assisted in the development of the Weatherly Waypoint Guides. I must, however, give special thanks to several who were particularly helpful. Dan Hale worked without a structure to follow, and produced the first books from little more than notes and a request to somehow get it done. Sheri Heckard refined Dan Hale's work to make later printings smoother, more consistent, and easier to use. Sheri also edited much of the material for style, consistency, and usability. Stacia Green relentlessly edited the listings and pointed out many areas for improvement. Jerry Kosciolek provided valuable insights during the early stages of the project. Don Douglass made a number of important suggestions.

Most especially, I recognize my lovely and enduring wife Marilynn, who put up with all the time I spent plotting waypoints, and then, regardless of the weather, ran the boat as we verified them. All that and wonderful meals, too. *Thank you Marilynn*.

Production: Sheri Heckard and Daniel Hale
Printed in U.S.A.

10 9 8 7 6 5 4

Published by Weatherly Press Division
Robert Hale & Co. Inc.
1803 132nd Ave. NE, Suite 4
Bellevue, WA 98005
U.S.A.
(206) 881-5212

ISBN 0-935727-10-8

Table of Contents

Introduction

This book contains more than 250 pre-plotted waypoints in the Gulf of Georgia. On the Vancouver Island side, the area includes the Gulf Islands, Lasqueti Island, and the waters north to Discovery Passage. On the east (mainland) side, the area includes the waters from Sarah Point to Point Roberts, including Jervis Inlet, Howe Sound, Burrard Inlet and Indian Arm. The waypoints are for use with both GPS and Loran-C electronic navigation equipment, and will make the navigator's job easier.

The waypoints were plotted on the latest editions of the largest scale charts available. Most of the waypoints have been verified by actually running to them by boat, a process that took about four weeks of steady work and resulted in a number of waypoints being relocated from their original plots. Since 1994, when this book was first published, further verification has taken place and a small number of additional waypoints have been added.

To prepare this guide, I assumed that my family and I were suddenly enveloped by fog, and as skipper I wanted a safe way to reach a safe destination. With safety in mind, many of the waypoints are not along the shortest possible routes, but rather are in open water, away from hazards. I have used very few buoy or beacon locations, since often they are close to hazards.

Waypoint locations were selected to serve several possible routes to the same destination. Do not assume, therefore, that you may go between any two waypoints safely. A rock, reef, or dry land may be in the way. Many landforms have been left off the maps, and hazards are not shown. Always do your original plotting on a chart. Use the waypoints in this book to help you be more accurate.

About waypoints

A waypoint is a specific place on earth's surface, located by latitude and longitude. A knowledgeable navigator can measure latitude and longitude fairly easily. It helps, however, if the navigator has a flat table, good light, and fair weather. Lack of experience or lack of good working conditions make the task more difficult. Yet without a good waypoint, GPS and Loran-C aren't very useful. They have to know where you want to go. Otherwise they can't tell you how to get there.

Used with up-to-date nautical charts, the waypoints in this book can help the navigator. First, use the appropriate nautical charts to plot the course to your destination, and choose desired locations for waypoints. Then find the map or maps in the book that show the area. Because the *Weatherly Waypoint Guide* was prepared with passagemaking in mind, it is probable that its waypoint locations will closely match your desired waypoints.

The waypoints are numbered generally from south to north on the Vancouver Island side, and north to south on the mainland side. Some numbers are skipped, so new waypoints can be added to future printings.

Note that the waypoints and maps are marked, "Reference only—not for navigation." The vessel's skipper retains full responsibility for navigation, and all course plots should be made independently of pre-plotted information.

About error

With all their numbers and authority, the waypoints in this book give the illusion of great precision. *Don't believe it.* Although the waypoints were plotted on the latest editions of the largest-scale charts available, the coordinates were rounded to the nearest 0.05′. Rounding creates a possible error of 150 feet of latitude and 100 feet of longitude. Remember too that the charts themselves can be wrong. Loran-C readings should be considered accurate only to a distance of about 100 meters—roughly the length of a football field. GPS, fortunately, is accurate to about 50 feet, often less. Differential GPS is all but spot-on accurate.

While GPS has eclipsed Loran-C for first-time accuracy, most of the time Loran-C will bring a boat remarkably close to a charted waypoint. Even so, until you have proven it on your boat and with your equipment, be cautious. Remember that GPS and Loran-C are tools, and that you should rely on no single tool when navigating. This book could be considered to be a tool, along with your charts, tide and current tables, compass, depth sounder, and radar. These tools, used with the aids to navigation—buoys, beacons, bells, whistles, horns, lights, ranges and such—all can help make for safe passages. *The wise skipper and navigator trusts no single tool or aid to navigation, but uses every available assist to run a safe course.*

About TDs

TDs are *Time Differences,* and apply to Loran-C only. The measuring of Time Differences in its radio signals is the means by which Loran-C determines location. Then, because in navigation we don't think in Time Differences, modern Loran-C receivers push the TDs through a program that calculates latitude and longitude. This TD-to-latitude-and-longitude conversion is a potential source of error with Loran-C.

Most modern Loran-C receivers display both latitude and longitude and Time Differences. If you wish to record TDs, a column is provided.

About the coordinates

The observant reader will see that the waypoint coordinates in this book are rounded to the nearest 0.05′, resulting in coordinates such as 48 23.00, 48 23.05, 48 23.10 and so forth. Having plotted more than a thousand waypoints and run nearly a thousand, I am satisfied that this accuracy will get most boats as close to their waypoint as can be done.

NAD 27 vs. NAD 83

All the waypoints in this book are adjusted to NAD 83, the North American Datum of 1983. Waypoints from the earlier NAD 27 charts are converted to NAD 83.

In this region, the 1983 survey moved latitudes south by approximately 61 feet (0.01′), and west by approximately 325 feet (0.08′). If the user plots a new waypoint on a NAD 27 chart, the plot can be converted to NAD 83 as follows:

Latitude
      48 24.60 NAD 27 latitude
        − 0.01 adjustment southward
      48 24.59 NAD 83 latitude (negligible change)

Longitude
      123 22.20 NAD 27 longitude
        + 0.08 adjustment westward
      123 22.28 NAD 83 longitude

In adjusting from NAD 27 to NAD 83 we have ignored the small change in latitude. The longitude change was rounded upward to 0.10′.

Cautionary note (Important)

While every effort has been made to assure that the information in this book is appropriate, *the user understands that the information is approximate only,* and should not be exclusively relied upon for navigation. It is possible that errors of calculation or typography have occurred, as well as errors in source materials. The user should not infer that the information in this book is a substitute for official maritime information contained on nautical charts, in the *List of Lights, Buoys and Fog Signals, Sailing Directions,* or *Notice to Shipping.* No waypoint should be considered dependable until verified by the user. The author and publisher do not warrant the accuracy of the information contained in this book, and assume no liability for its use. Furthermore, since they have no control over weather and sea conditions, and have no knowledge of the user's intended courses, the author and publisher make no claims for the suitability of the waypoints for any purpose.

—*Robert Hale*

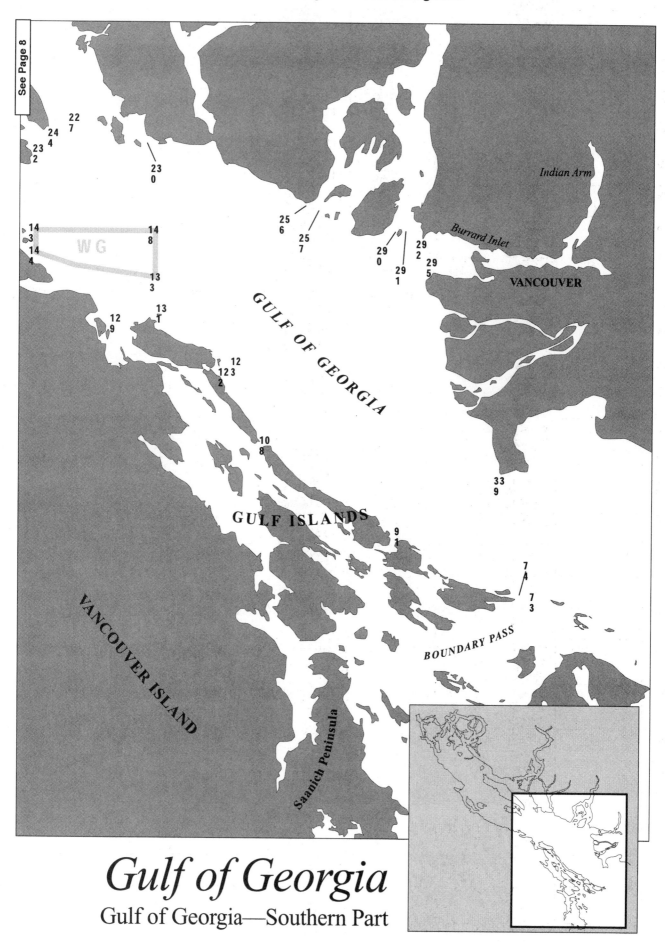

See Page 8

22
7

24
4

23
2

23
0

14
3

14
4

W G

14
8

13
3

13
1

12
9

12
2

12
3
2

10
8

25
6

25
7

29
0

29
1

29
2

29
5

GULF OF GEORGIA

Indian Arm

Burrard Inlet

VANCOUVER

33
9

9
1

7
4

7
3

GULF ISLANDS

BOUNDARY PASS

VANCOUVER ISLAND

Saanich Peninsula

Gulf of Georgia
Gulf of Georgia—Southern Part

Waypoint	Ship's Waypoint	Description	Latitude/ Longitude	TD1/ TD2 For Loran Only	Notes
73		Boundary Pass, E entrance	48 46.90 123 00.70		
74		Tumbo Channel, S entrance	48 47.70 123 02.30		
91		Active Pass, N entrance	48 53.50 123 18.00		
108		Porlier Pass, NE entrance	49 01.35 123 34.90		
122		Gabriola Passage, SE entrance	49 07.20 123 40.70		
123		Thrasher Rock	49 09.00 123 38.55		
129		Fairway Channel, middle, 0.3 mi S of Snake Island Reef light & bell buoy P2	49 12.20 123 53.15		
131		Entrance Island, 0.25 mi N of	49 12.80 123 48.40		
133		Whiskey-Golf, SE corner	49 14.83 123 48.40		
143		Whiskey-Golf, NW corner, off Ballenas Islands	49 21.35 124 07.70		
144		Whiskey-Golf, SW corner, S of Ballenas Islands	49 19.35 124 07.70		
148		Whiskey-Golf, NE corner, off Halibut Bank	49 21.00 123 48.40		
227		Malaspina Strait, S entrance	49 30.00 124 04.95		
230		Welcome Passage, S entrance, E of Merry Island	49 28.00 123 53.80		
232		Squitty Bay, entrance, 0.25 mi S of	49 27.00 124 09.40		
244		Upwood Point, 0.25 mi SE of	49 29.25 124 07.20		
256		Gower Point, 0.25 mi S of	49 22.75 123 32.20		
257		Barfleur Passage, W entrance	49 22.30 123 30.45		
290		Queen Charlotte Channel, entrance, between Point Cowan & Passage Island	49 20.20 123 20.25		
291		Queen Charlotte Channel, S entrance, between Passage Island & Point Atkinson	49 20.00 123 17.50		
292		Point Atkinson, 0.25 mi S of	49 19.60 123 16.00		
295		Spanish Bank, 0.25 mi N of	49 17.60 123 15.10		
339		Point Roberts, 0.25 mi S of	48 58.00 123 05.30		

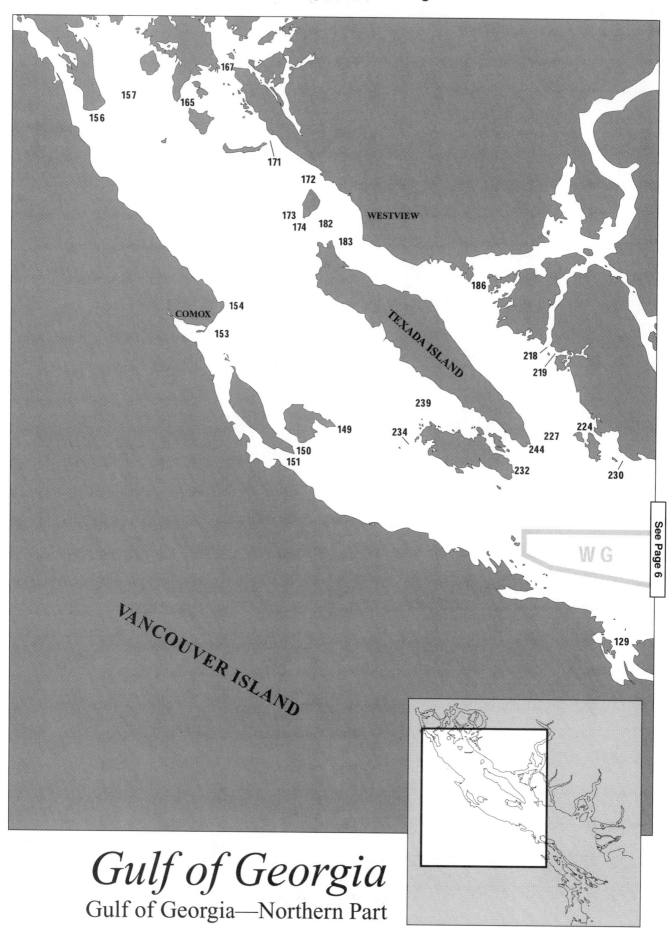

167

157

165

156

171

172

173
174   182

WESTVIEW

183

186

COMOX   154

153

TEXADA ISLAND

218

219

239

149   234

227   224

150   244

151   232   230

129

See Page 6

W G

Gulf of Georgia
Gulf of Georgia—Northern Part

VANCOUVER ISLAND

Waypoint	Ship's Waypoint	Description	Latitude/ Longitude	TD1/ TD2 *For Loran Only*	Notes
129		Fairway Channel, middle, 0.3 mi S of Snake Island Reef light & bell buoy P2	49 12.20 123 53.15		
149		Hornby Island, 1 mi SE of St. John Point	49 30.60 124 33.65		
150		Lambert Channel, S entrance	49 28.55 124 39.75		
151		Baynes Sound, entrance, mid-channel	49 28.00 124 41.30		
153		Comox Bar light and bell buoy P54	49 39.50 124 51.70		
154		East Cardinal buoy PJ, 1.5 mi SE of Cape Lazo	49 41.50 124 49.70		
156		Discovery Passage, entrance, S of Cape Mudge Sector light	49 59.75 125 11.90		
157		Sutil Channel, S entrance, middle	50 01.00 125 06.00		
165		Baker Passage, middle, between Twin Islands & Spilsbury Point	50 00.70 124 56.30		
167		Sarah Point, 0.25 mi W of	50 03.80 124 51.00		
171		Savary Island, E of, mid-channel between Mace Point and Hurtado Point	49 57.40 124 45.40		
172		Shearwater Passage, N entrance	49 54.30 124 40.70		
173		Shearwater Passage, S entrance, 0.5 mi W of Vivian Island	49 50.70 124 42.95		
174		Algerine Passage, W entrance	49 49.30 124 41.25		
182		Algerine Passage, E entrance	49 49.70 124 37.20		
183		Malaspina Strait, N entrance, between Grilse Point & Grief Point	49 48.20 124 33.70		
186		Jervis Inlet, entrance	49 44.10 124 14.85		
218		Agamemnon Channel, S entrance	49 38.35 124 05.10		
219		Pender Harbour, entrance, between Henry Point & Williams Island	49 37.85 124 03.75		
224		Welcome Passage, N entrance	49 31.30 123 58.95		
227		Malaspina Strait, S entrance	49 30.00 124 04.95		
230		Welcome Passage, S entrance, E of Merry Island	49 28.00 123 53.80		
232		Squitty Bay, entrance, 0.25 mi S of	49 27.00 124 09.40		
234		Stevens Passage, middle, E of Sisters Islets	49 29.30 124 24.80		
239		Sabine Channel, W entrance	49 33.40 124 22.55		
244		Upwood Point, 0.25 mi SE of	49 29.25 124 07.20		

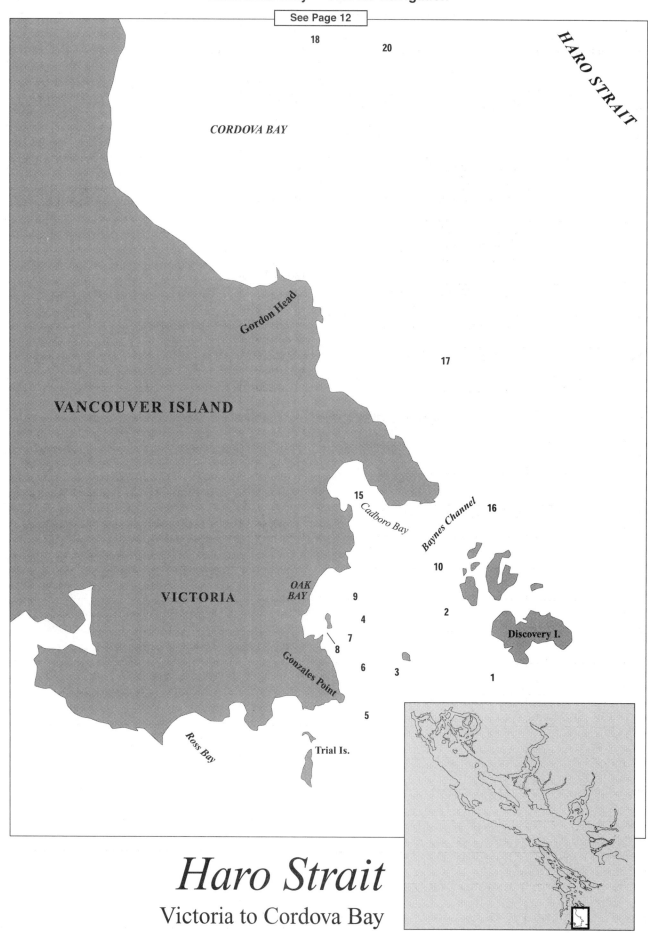

See Page 12

18

20

HARO STRAIT

CORDOVA BAY

Gordon Head

17

VANCOUVER ISLAND

15

Cadboro Bay

16

Baynes Channel

10

VICTORIA

OAK BAY

9

2

4

Discovery I.

7

8

6

3

1

Gonzales Point

5

Ross Bay

Trial Is.

Haro Strait

Victoria to Cordova Bay

Waypoint	Ship's Waypoint	Description	Latitude/ Longitude	TD1/ TD2 *For Loran Only*	Notes
1		Plumper Passage, S entrance, middle	48 25.00 123 14.86		
2		Plumper Passage, N entrance, middle	48 25.75 123 15.80		
3		Mayor Channel, S entrance, middle	48 25.00 123 16.80		
4		Mayor Channel, 0.2 mi SSW of Fiddle Reef	48 25.50 123 17.10		
5		Gonzales Point, 0.4 mi SE of	48 24.50 123 17.10		
6		Mouat Channel, center, between Thames Shoal & buoy V25	48 25.10 123 17.20		
7		Harris Island, 0.1 mi W of	48 25.40 123 17.50		
8		Oak Bay Marina, entrance	48 25.50 123 17.95		
9		Tod Rock, 0.1 mi WNW of	48 25.90 123 17.40		
10		Baynes Channel, S entrance	48 26.30 123 16.10		
15		Cadboro Bay, middle	48 27.20 123 17.40		
16		Baynes Channel, N entrance	48 27.00 123 15.05		
17		Johnstone Reef, 0.5 mi E of	48 28.70 123 15.90		
18		Zero Rock, 0.5 mi W of	48 31.50 123 18.30		
20		Zero Rock, 0.5 mi E of	48 31.40 123 16.80		

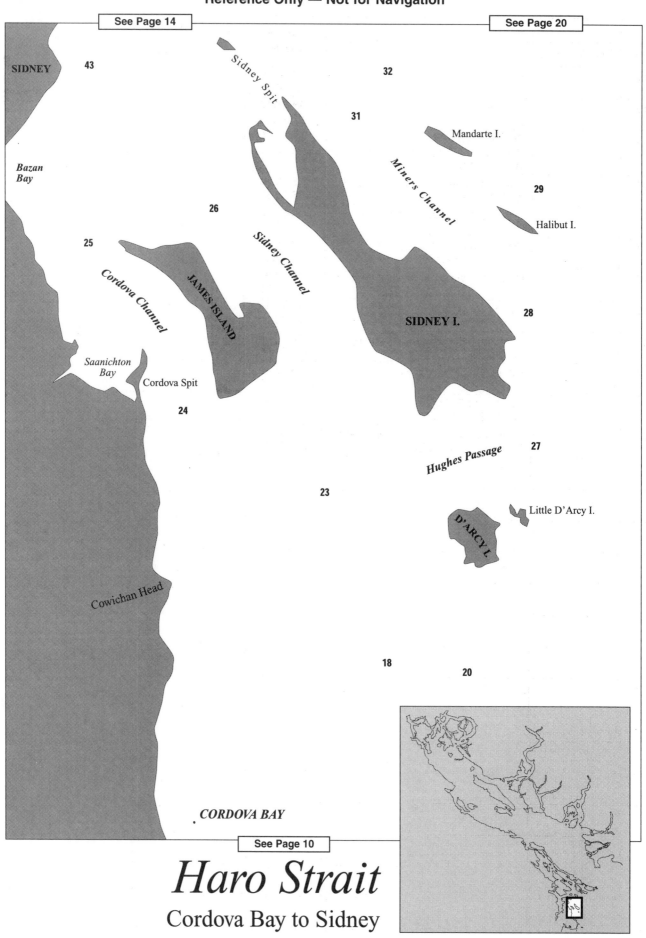

See Page 14

See Page 20

SIDNEY

43

Sidney Spit

32

31

Mandarte I.

Bazan Bay

26

Miners Channel

29

Halibut I.

25

Cordova Channel

JAMES ISLAND

Sidney Channel

SIDNEY I.

28

Saanichton Bay

Cordova Spit

24

27

Hughes Passage

23

Little D'Arcy I.

D'ARCY I.

Cowichan Head

18

20

See Page 10

CORDOVA BAY

Haro Strait

Cordova Bay to Sidney

Waypoint	Ship's Waypoint	Description	Latitude/ Longitude	TD1/ TD2 *For Loran Only*	Notes
18		Zero Rock, 0.5 mi W of	48 31.50 123 18.30		
20		Zero Rock, 0.5 mi E of	48 31.40 123 16.80		
23		Sidney Channel, S entrance, Hughes Passage, W entrance, clear of D'Arcy Shoals	48 34.50 123 18.80		
24		Cordova Channel, middle, SW of S tip of James Island	48 35.20 123 21.60		
25		James Island, 0.25 mi W of N tip	48 37.10 123 23.20		
26		Sidney Channel, N entrance, 0.25 mi W of Sidney Channel light buoy U2	48 37.50 123 21.10		
27		Hughes Passage, E entrance	48 34.90 123 15.70		
28		Miners Channel, S entrance	48 36.40 123 15.80		
29		Mandarte Island East Cardinal light buoy UT	48 37.60 123 16.00		
31		Miners Channel, mid-way	48 38.50 123 18.90		
32		South Cod Reef South Cardinal light buoy US, 0.25 mi SW of	48 38.90 123 18.40		
43		Approach to Port Sidney breakwater, between Marks U5 & U6	48 39.00 123 23.20		

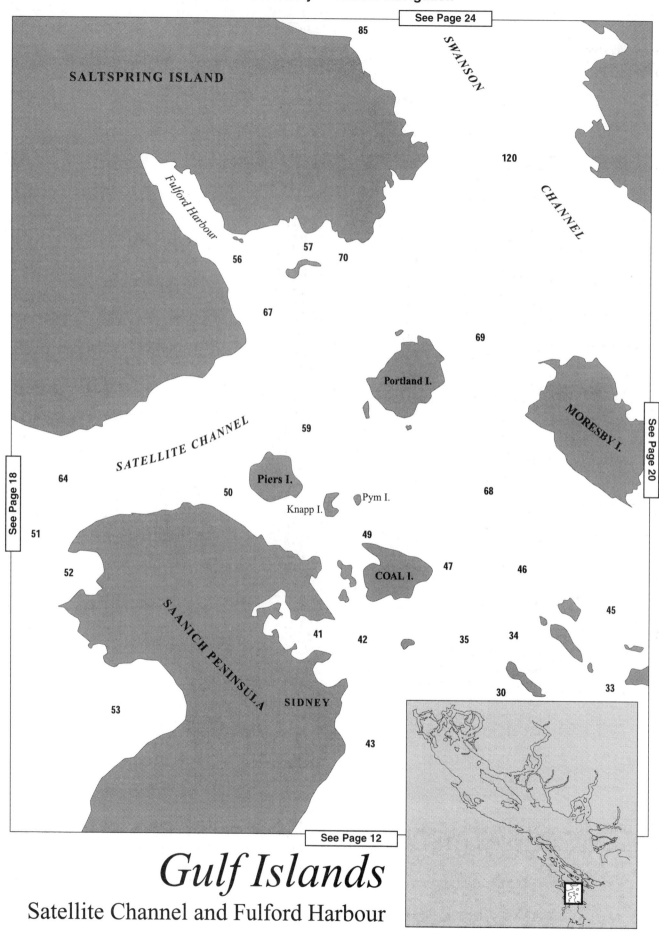

See Page 24

85

SWANSON

120

CHANNEL

SALTSPRING ISLAND

Fulford Harbour

57

56

70

67

69

Portland I.

59

MORESBY I.

See Page 20

SATELLITE CHANNEL

64

Piers I.

50

Knapp I.

Pym I.

68

See Page 18

51

49

52

47

46

COAL I.

45

41

42

35

34

SAANICH PENINSULA

SIDNEY

53

30

33

43

See Page 12

Gulf Islands

Satellite Channel and Fulford Harbour

Waypoint	Ship's Waypoint	Description	Latitude/ Longitude	TD1/ TD2 *For Loran Only*	Notes
30		Miners Channel, N entrance	48 39.60 123 20.50		
33		Gooch Island, 0.25 mi W of W tip	48 39.65 123 18.45		
34		Mid-channel between NW tips of Forrest Island & Domville Island	48 40.30 123 20.30		
35		Dock Island, 0.2 mi ESE of	48 40.20 123 21.20		
41		Tsehum Harbour light	48 40.30 123 24.25		
42		Mid-channel between Armstrong Point & Little Shell Island	48 40.15 123 23.20		
43		Approach to Port Sidney breakwater, between Marks U5 & U6	48 39.00 123 23.20		
45		Approach to passage between Brethour Island & Comet Island	48 40.65 123 18.30		
46		Reay Island, 0.25 mi NW of	48 41.15 123 20.10		
47		Charmer Point, 0.25 mi E of	48 41.15 123 21.50		
49		Colburne Passage, entrance, 0.1 mi N of Fir Cone Point	48 41.55 123 23.25		
50		Colburne Passage, W entrance	48 42.00 123 25.80		
51		Saanich Inlet, entrance, 0.5 mi WNW of Moses Point	48 41.60 123 29.80		
52		Saanich Inlet, Deep Cove entrance	48 41.00 123 29.20		
53		Saanich Inlet, Patricia Bay entrance	48 39.30 123 28.40		
56		Fulford Harbour, 0.2 mi SSE of Jackson Rock	48 45.00 123 25.75		
57		Fulford Harbour, 0.2 mi N of Russell Island	48 45.20 123 24.40		
59		Shute Passage, W entrance	48 42.90 123 24.45		
64		Satellite Channel, between Cape Keppel & Moses Point	48 42.20 123 29.30		
67		Fulford Harbour, entrance, between Russell Island & Isabella Point	48 44.40 123 25.00		
68		Confluence of Shute Passage, Moresby Passage, Prevost Passage	48 42.15 123 20.80		
69		Moresby Passage, 0.3 mi W of Canoe Rock	48 44.10 123 20.80		
70		Fulford Harbour, entrance, between Russell Island & Eleanor Point	48 45.00 123 23.70		
85		Captain Passage, between Yeo Point and Channel Islands	48 47.85 123 23.35		
120		Swanson Channel, between Beaver Point & Thieves Bay	48 46.25 123 20.60		

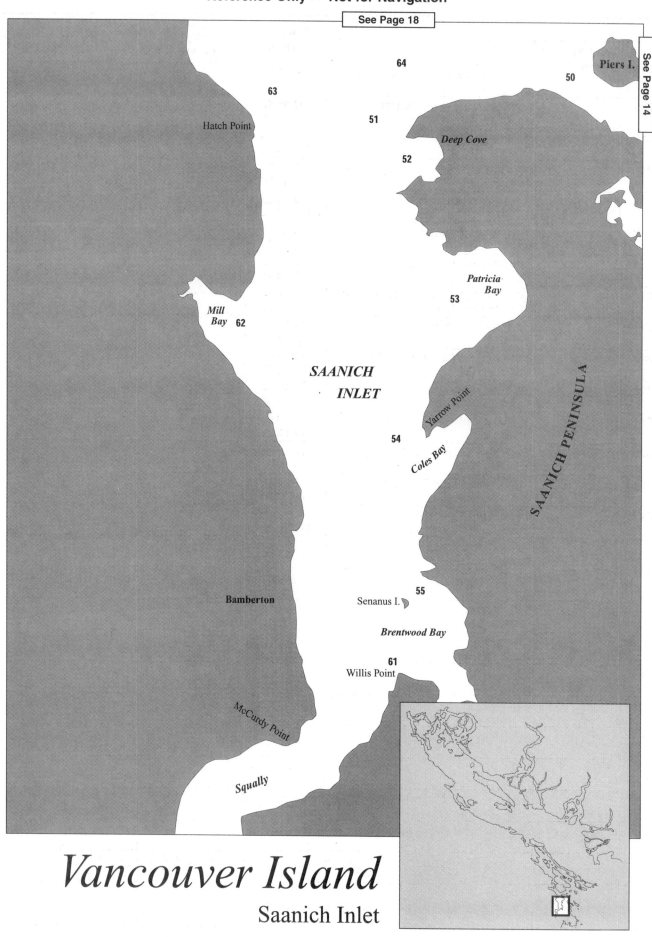

See Page 18

See Page 14

Piers I.

50

64

63

51

Hatch Point

Deep Cove

52

Patricia Bay

53

Mill Bay 62

SAANICH INLET

Yarrow Point

54

Coles Bay

SAANICH PENINSULA

Bamberton

55

Senanus I.

Brentwood Bay

61

Willis Point

McCurdy Point

Squally

Vancouver Island

Saanich Inlet

Waypoint	Ship's Waypoint	Description	Latitude/ Longitude	TD1/ TD2 For Loran Only	Notes
50		Colburne Passage, W entrance	48 42.00 123 25.80		
51		Saanich Inlet, entrance, 0.5 mi WNW of Moses Point	48 41.60 123 29.80		
52		Saanich Inlet, Deep Cove entrance	48 41.00 123 29.20		
53		Saanich Inlet, Patricia Bay entrance	48 39.30 123 28.40		
54		Saanich Inlet, buoy U23, off Dyer Rocks, 0.25 mi NW of	48 37.60 123 29.50		
55		Brentwood Bay, N entrance	48 35.70 123 28.95		
61		Brentwood Bay, S entrance, 0.1 mi NNW of Willis Point	48 34.75 123 29.30		
62		Saanich Inlet, entrance to Mill Bay	48 39.00 123 32.40		
63		Saanich Inlet, entrance, between Hatch Point & Patey Rock	48 41.90 123 31.70		
64		Satellite Channel, between Cape Keppel & Moses Point	48 42.20 123 29.30		

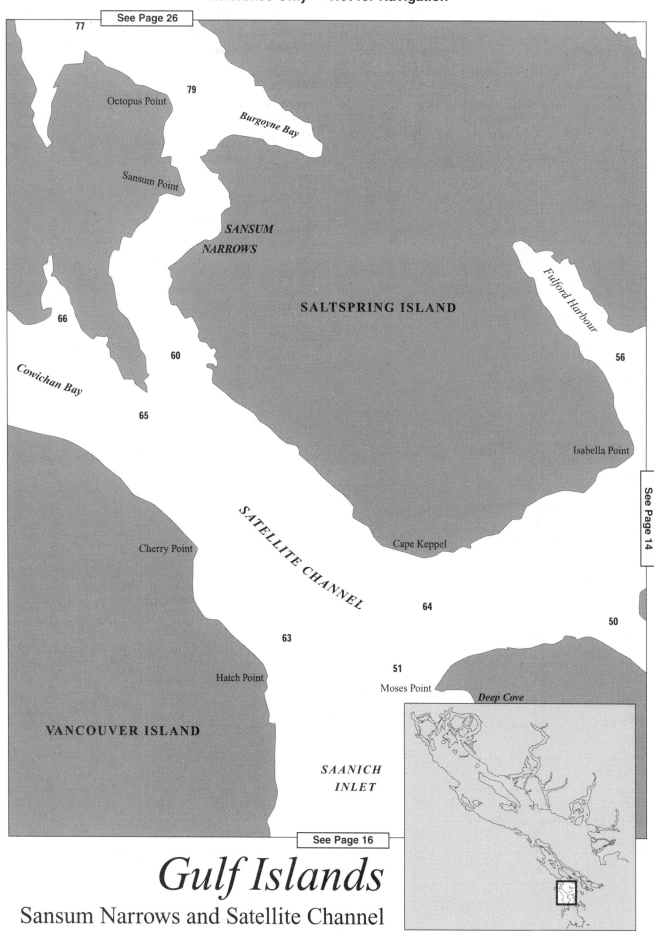

See Page 26

77

79

Octopus Point

Burgoyne Bay

Sansum Point

SANSUM NARROWS

SALTSPRING ISLAND

Fulford Harbour

66

60

56

Cowichan Bay

65

Isabella Point

See Page 14

SATELLITE CHANNEL

Cherry Point

Cape Keppel

64

50

63

51

Hatch Point

Moses Point

Deep Cove

VANCOUVER ISLAND

SAANICH INLET

See Page 16

Gulf Islands

Sansum Narrows and Satellite Channel

Waypoint	Ship's Waypoint	Description	Latitude/ Longitude	TD1/ TD2 *For Loran Only*	Notes
50		Colburne Passage, W entrance	48 42.00 123 25.80		
51		Saanich Inlet, entrance, 0.5 mi WNW of Moses Point	48 41.60 123 29.80		
56		Fulford Harbour, 0.2 mi SSE of Jackson Rock	48 45.00 123 25.75		
60		Sansum Narrows, S entrance	48 45.00 123 33.65		
63		Saanich Inlet, entrance, between Hatch Point & Patey Rock	48 41.90 123 31.70		
64		Satellite Channel, between Cape Keppel & Moses Point	48 42.20 123 29.30		
65		Cowichan Bay, entrance	48 44.40 123 34.30		
66		Genoa Bay, entrance	48 45.45 123 35.70		
77		Maple Bay, entrance	48 48.60 123 35.40		
79		Sansum Narrows, 500 yards E of Octopus Point	48 48.00 123 33.40		

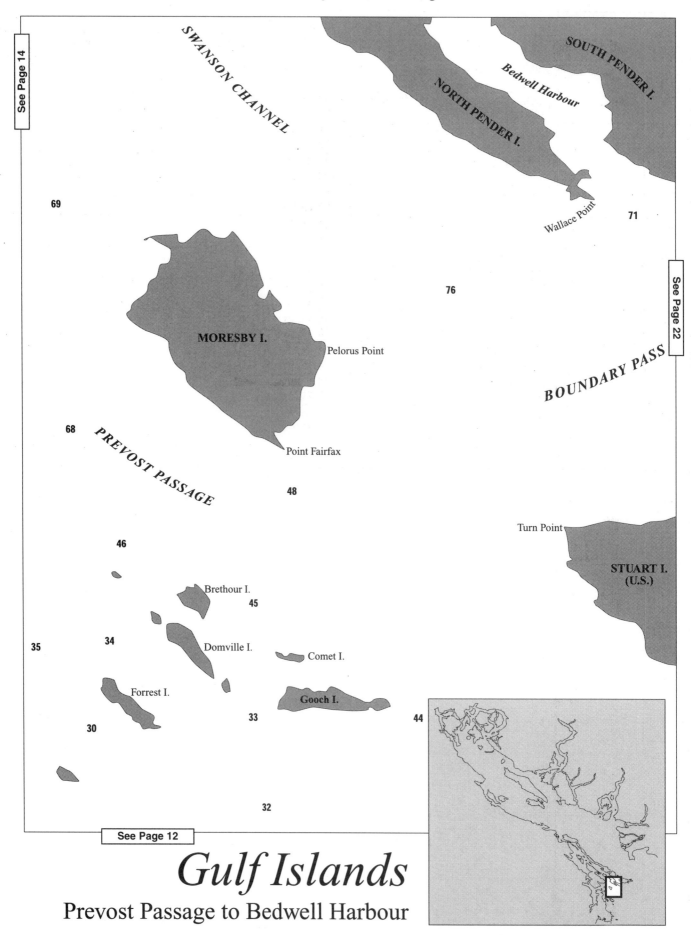

SWANSON CHANNEL

SOUTH PENDER I.

Bedwell Harbour

NORTH PENDER I.

69

Wallace Point

71

76

MORESBY I.

Pelorus Point

68

PREVOST PASSAGE

Point Fairfax

48

BOUNDARY PASS

Turn Point

STUART I. (U.S.)

46

Brethour I.

45

34

Domville I.

Comet I.

35

Forrest I.

Gooch I.

30

33

44

32

See Page 14

See Page 22

See Page 12

Gulf Islands
Prevost Passage to Bedwell Harbour

Waypoint	Ship's Waypoint	Description	Latitude/ Longitude	TD1/ TD2 *For Loran Only*	Notes
30		Miners Channel, N entrance	48 39.60 123 20.50		
32		South Cod Reef South Cardinal light buoy US, 0.25 mi SW of	48 38.90 123 18.40		
33		Gooch Island, 0.25 mi W of W tip	48 39.65 123 18.45		
34		Mid-channel between NW tips of Forrest Island & Domville Island	48 40.30 123 20.30		
35		Dock Island, 0.2 mi ESE of	48 40.20 123 21.20		
44		Tom Point, 0.25 mi E of	48 39.70 123 16.10		
45		Approach to passage between Brethour Island & Comet Island	48 40.65 123 18.30		
46		Reay Island, 0.25 mi NW of	48 41.15 123 20.10		
48		Prevost Passage, between Point Fairfax & Arachne Reef	48 41.50 123 17.90		
68		Confluence of Shute Passage, Moresby Passage, Prevost Passage	48 42.15 123 20.80		
69		Moresby Passage, 0.3 mi W of Canoe Rock	48 44.10 123 20.80		
71		Bedwell Harbour, entrance	48 44.10 123 13.40		
76		Swanson Channel, middle, S entrance	48 43.40 123 15.90		

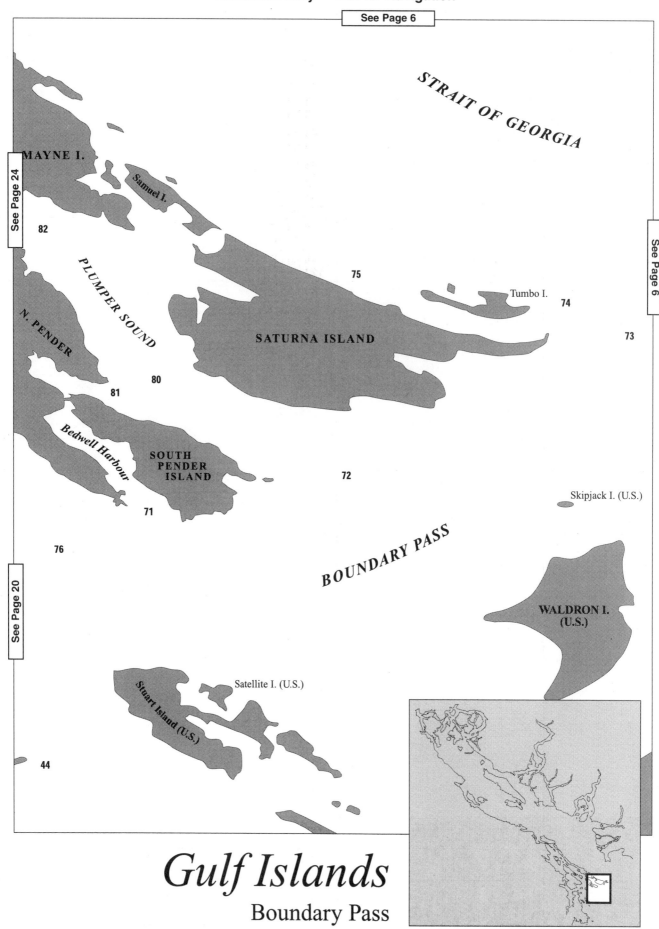

See Page 6

See Page 24

See Page 6

See Page 20

STRAIT OF GEORGIA

MAYNE I.

Samuel I.

82

PLUMPER SOUND

75

Tumbo I.

74

73

N. PENDER

SATURNA ISLAND

80

81

Bedwell Harbour

SOUTH PENDER ISLAND

72

Skipjack I. (U.S.)

71

76

BOUNDARY PASS

WALDRON I. (U.S.)

Satellite I. (U.S.)

Stuart Island (U.S.)

44

Gulf Islands
Boundary Pass

Waypoint	Ship's Waypoint	Description	Latitude/ Longitude	TD1/ TD2 *For Loran Only*	Notes
44		Tom Point, 0.25 mi E of	48 39.70 123 16.10		
71		Bedwell Harbour, entrance	48 44.10 123 13.40		
72		Plumper Sound, S entrance	48 45.00 123 08.10		
73		Boundary Pass, E entrance	48 46.90 123 00.70		
74		Tumbo Channel, S entrance	48 47.70 123 02.30		
75		Tumbo Channel, N entrance	48 48.20 123 07.90		
76		Swanson Channel, middle, S entrance	48 43.40 123 15.90		
80		Plumper Sound, mid-channel between Croker Point & Razor Point	48 46.40 123 13.00		
81		Port Browning, entrance	48 46.05 123 14.15		
82		Navy Channel, E entrance	48 48.90 123 16.00		

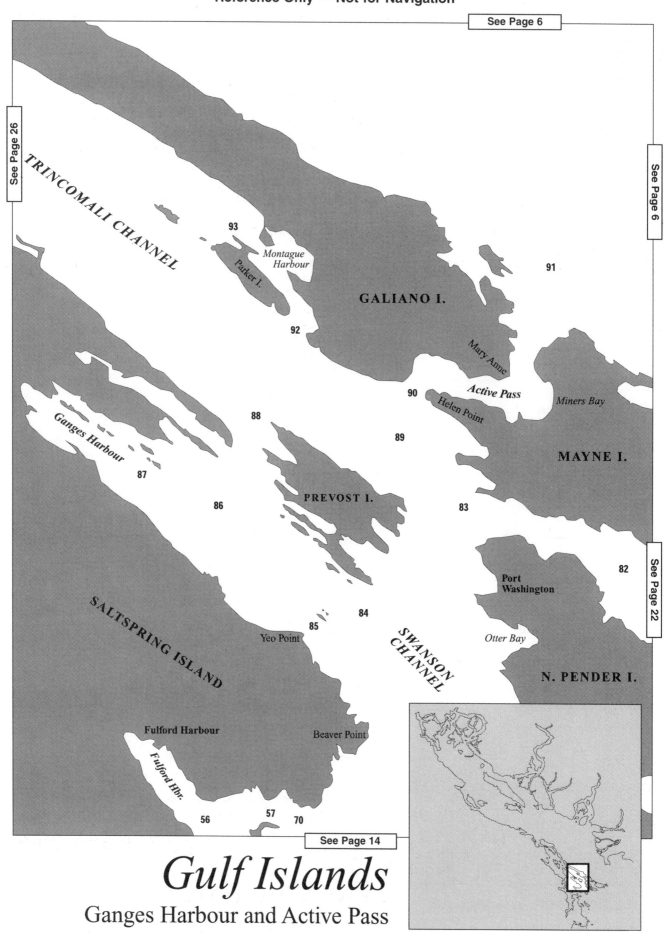

See Page 6

See Page 26

See Page 6

TRINCOMALI CHANNEL

93

Montague Harbour

Parker I.

92

GALIANO I.

91

Mary Anne

Active Pass

90

Helen Point

Miners Bay

88

Ganges Harbour

89

MAYNE I.

87

86

PREVOST I.

83

See Page 22

82

Port Washington

84

85

Yeo Point

SWANSON CHANNEL

Otter Bay

SALTSPRING ISLAND

N. PENDER I.

Fulford Harbour

Beaver Point

Fulford Hbr.

56

57

70

See Page 14

Gulf Islands

Ganges Harbour and Active Pass

Waypoint	Ship's Waypoint	Description	Latitude/ Longitude	TD1/ TD2 *For Loran Only*	Notes
56		Fulford Harbour, 0.2 mi SSE of Jackson Rock	48 45.00 123 25.75		
57		Fulford Harbour, 0.2 mi N of Russell Island	48 45.20 123 24.40		
70		Fulford Harbour, entrance, between Russell Island & Eleanor Point	48 45.00 123 23.70		
82		Navy Channel, E entrance	48 48.90 123 16.00		
83		Navy Channel, W entrance	48 50.00 123 20.00		
84		Captain Passage, E entrance, 0.3 mi S of Point Liddell	48 48.20 123 22.15		
85		Captain Passage, between Yeo Point and Channel Islands	48 47.85 123 23.35		
86		Captain Passage, 0.5 mi SE of Horda Shoals light buoy UD	48 49.45 123 25.55		
87		Ganges Harbour, entrance	48 50.10 123 27.30		
88		Captain Passage, N entrance	48 51.15 123 24.75		
89		Enterprise Reef, 0.4 mi SW of	48 50.55 123 21.45		
90		Active Pass, W entrance	48 51.45 123 21.05		
91		Active Pass, N entrance	48 53.50 123 18.00		
92		Montague Harbour, S entrance	48 52.30 123 23.70		
93		Montague Harbour, NW entrance	48 53.90 123 25.20		

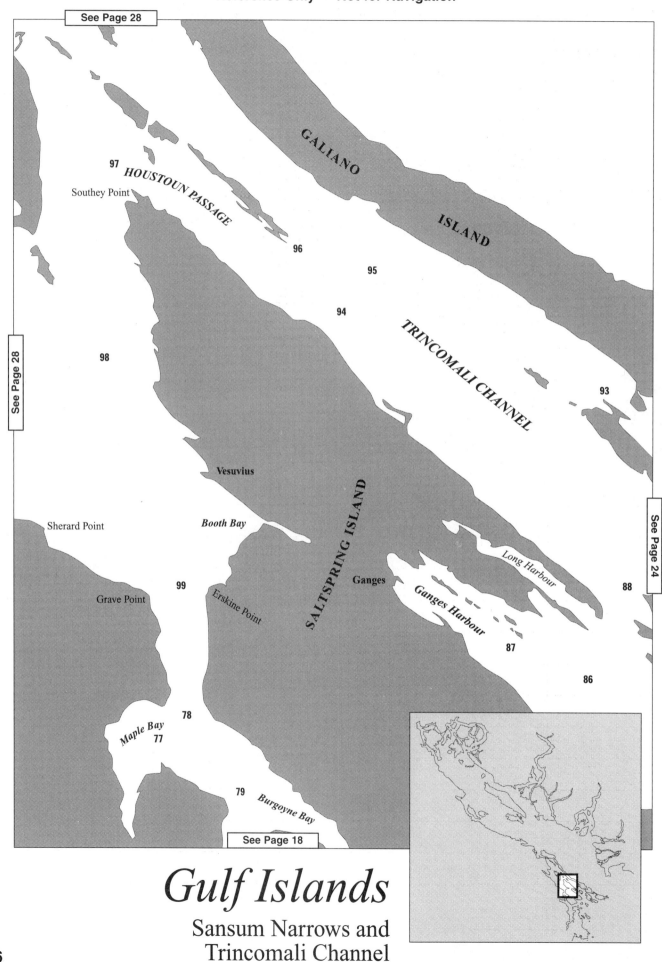

See Page 28

See Page 28

See Page 24

See Page 18

97

HOUSTOUN PASSAGE

Southey Point

GALIANO

ISLAND

96

95

94

TRINCOMALI CHANNEL

93

98

Vesuvius

Booth Bay

SALTSPRING ISLAND

Long Harbour

88

Sherard Point

Ganges

Ganges Harbour

99

Erskine Point

87

Grave Point

86

78

Maple Bay

77

79

Burgoyne Bay

Gulf Islands

Sansum Narrows and
Trincomali Channel

26

Waypoint	Ship's Waypoint	Description	Latitude/ Longitude	TD1/ TD2 *For Loran Only*	Notes
77		Maple Bay, entrance	48 48.60 123 35.40		
78		Sansum Narrows, off Maple Bay entrance	48 49.15 123 34.70		
79		Sansum Narrows, 500 yards E of Octopus Point	48 48.00 123 33.40		
86		Captain Passage, 0.5 mi SE of Horda Shoals light buoy UD	48 49.45 123 25.55		
87		Ganges Harbour, entrance	48 50.10 123 27.30		
88		Captain Passage, N entrance	48 51.15 123 24.75		
93		Montague Harbour, NW entrance	48 53.90 123 25.20		
94		Trincomali Channel, between Victoria Shoal & Victoria Rock	48 55.00 123 31.15		
95		Trincomali Channel, between Walker Rock & Victoria Shoal	48 55.40 123 30.20		
96		Panther Point, Wallace Island, 0.25 mi SE of	48 55.70 123 31.80		
97		Houstoun Passage, 0.5 mi W of Southey Point	48 57.10 123 36.40		
98		Houstoun Passage, S entrance	48 54.35 123 36.75		
99		Sansum Narrows, N entrance	48 51.10 123 34.95		

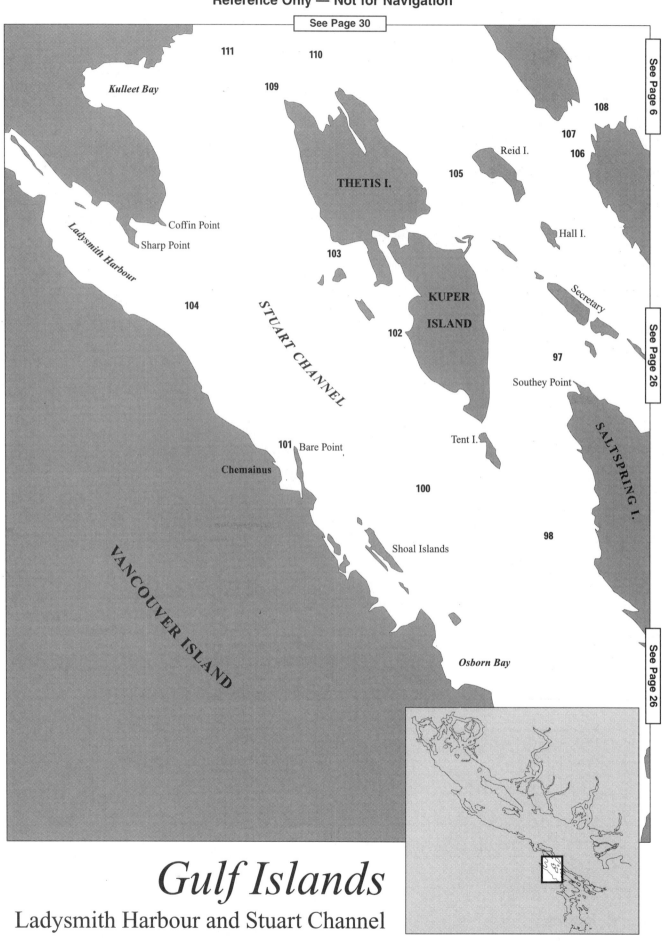

See Page 30

See Page 6

See Page 26

See Page 26

111

110

109

108

107

106

Kulleet Bay

Reid I.

105

THETIS I.

Hall I.

Coffin Point

Secretary

Sharp Point

103

Ladysmith Harbour

KUPER ISLAND

97

104

STUART CHANNEL

102

Southey Point

Tent I.

101

Bare Point

Chemainus

100

SALTSPRING I.

VANCOUVER ISLAND

Shoal Islands

98

Osborn Bay

Gulf Islands
Ladysmith Harbour and Stuart Channel

Waypoint	Ship's Waypoint	Description	Latitude/ Longitude	TD1/ TD2 *For Loran Only*	Notes
97		Houstoun Passage, 0.5 mi W of Southey Point	48 57.10 123 36.40		
98		Houstoun Passage, S entrance	48 54.35 123 36.75		
100		Stuart Channel, middle, S of Tent Island	48 55.00 123 39.10		
101		Chemainus Bay, entrance	48 55.85 123 42.60		
102		Telegraph Harbour, entrance	48 57.40 123 40.15		
103		Preedy Harbour, NW entrance	48 58.80 123 41.60		
104		Ladysmith Harbour, entrance	48 58.10 123 45.10		
105		Trincomali Channel, between Reid Island & Thetis Island	49 00.00 123 38.70		
106		Porlier Pass, SW entrance	49 00.25 123 35.65		
107		Porlier Pass, W entrance	49 00.55 123 35.15		
108		Porlier Pass, NE entrance	49 01.35 123 34.90		
109		Fraser Point, Thetis Island, 0.25 mi NW of	49 01.35 123 42.90		
110		Ragged Islets, 0.25 mi W of	49 01.80 123 42.00		
111		Stuart Channel, between Fraser Point & Yellow Point	49 01.85 123 43.90		

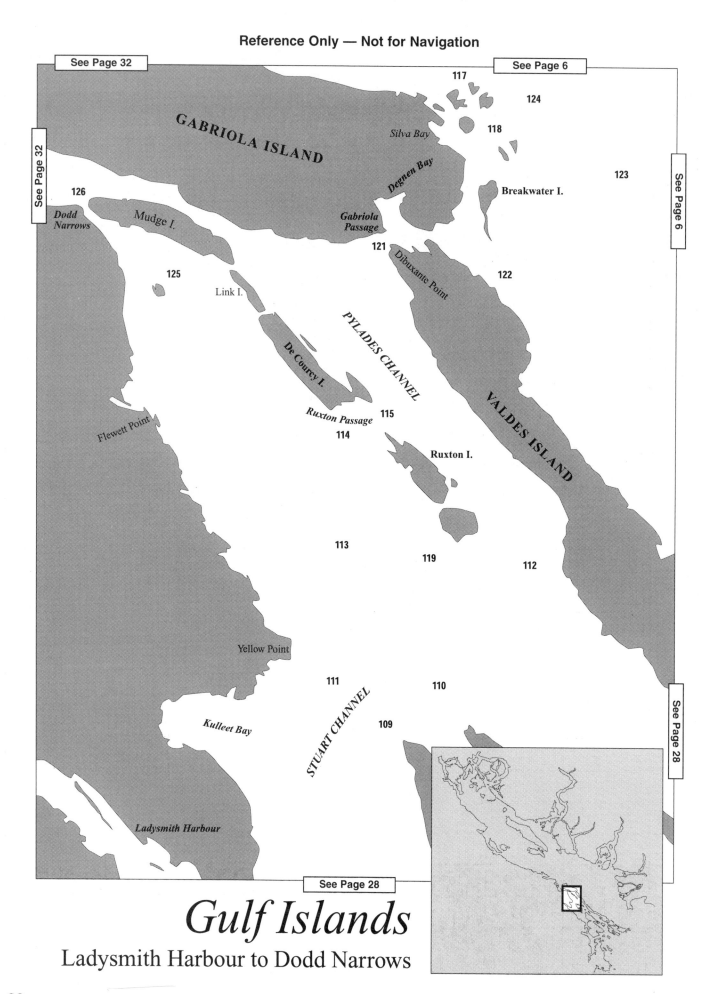

See Page 32

See Page 6

117

124

Silva Bay

118

GABRIOLA ISLAND

See Page 32

See Page 6

123

Breakwater I.

126

Dodd Narrows

Mudge I.

Degnen Bay

Gabriola Passage

121

Dibuxante Point

122

125

Link I.

De Courcy I.

PYLADES CHANNEL

VALDES ISLAND

Flewett Point

Ruxton Passage

115

114

Ruxton I.

113

119

112

Yellow Point

111

110

STUART CHANNEL

109

Kulleet Bay

Ladysmith Harbour

See Page 28

See Page 28

Gulf Islands

Ladysmith Harbour to Dodd Narrows

Waypoint	Ship's Waypoint	Description	Latitude/ Longitude	TD1/ TD2 *For Loran Only*	Notes
109		Fraser Point, Thetis Island, 0.25 mi NW of	**49 01.35** 123 42.90		
110		Ragged Islets, 0.25 mi W of	**49 01.80** 123 42.00		
111		Stuart Channel, between Fraser Point & Yellow Point	**49 01.85** 123 43.90		
112		Pylades Channel, SE entrance	**49 03.40** 123 40.50		
113		Stuart Channel, middle, NW of Danger Reefs	**49 03.65** 123 43.95		
114		Ruxton Passage, W entrance	**49 05.25** 123 43.90		
115		Ruxton Passage, NE entrance	**49 05.45** 123 42.95		
117		Commodore Passage, Flat Top Islands, N entrance	**49 09.70** 123 41.55		
118		Commodore Passage, Flat Top Islands, S entrance	**49 09.00** 123 40.85		
119		Stuart Channel, between Danger Reefs & Tree Island	**49 03.45** 123 42.30		
121		Gabriola Passage, W entrance	**49 07.60** 123 43.25		
122		Gabriola Passage, SE entrance	**49 07.20** 123 40.70		
123		Thrasher Rock	**49 09.00** 123 38.55		
124		Flat Top Islands, E entrance, 0.3 mi E of Brant Reef	**49 09.45** 123 40.10		
125		Round Island, 0.25 mi NNE of	**49 07.25** 123 47.55		
126		Northumberland Channel, approach to Dodd Narrows	**49 08.30** 123 49.15		

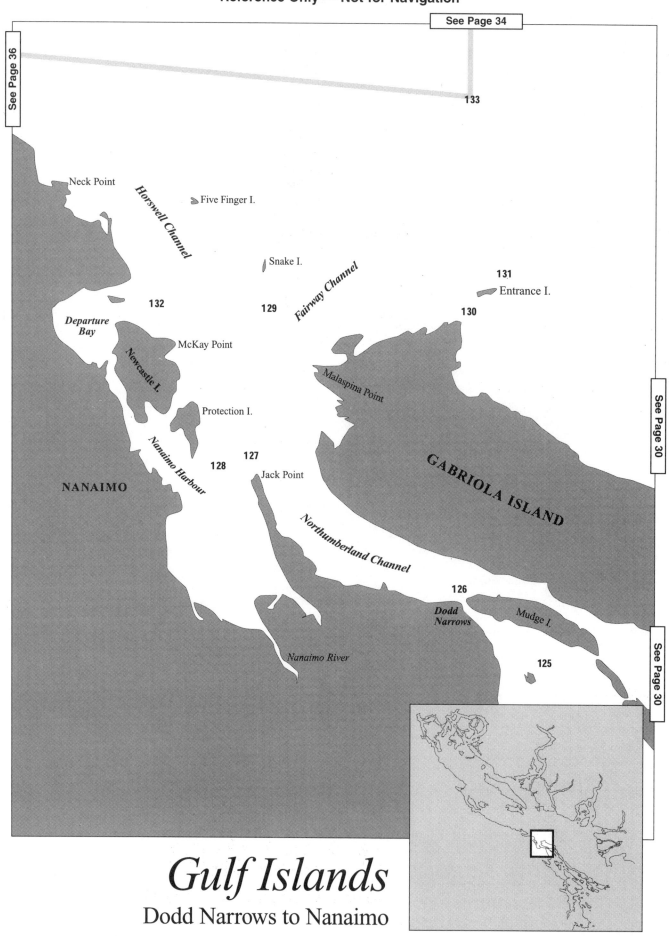

See Page 34

See Page 36

133

Neck Point

Five Finger I.

Horswell Channel

Snake I.

131

Entrance I.

132

129

Fairway Channel

130

Departure Bay

McKay Point

Malaspina Point

Newcastle I.

Protection I.

GABRIOLA ISLAND

See Page 30

128

127

Nanaimo Harbour

Jack Point

NANAIMO

Northumberland Channel

126

Dodd Narrows

Mudge I.

125

Nanaimo River

See Page 30

Gulf Islands
Dodd Narrows to Nanaimo

Waypoint	Ship's Waypoint	Description	Latitude/ Longitude	TD1/ TD2 *For Loran Only*	Notes
125		Round Island, 0.25 mi NNE of	49 07.25 123 47.55		
126		Northumberland Channel, approach to Dodd Narrows	49 08.30 123 49.15		
127		Jack Point, 0.25 mi N of	49 10.30 123 53.70		
128		McKay Channel, entrance	49 10.15 123 54.75		
129		Fairway Channel, middle, 0.3 mi S of Snake Island Reef light & bell buoy P2	49 12.20 123 53.15		
130		Forwood Channel, middle	49 12.25 123 49.00		
131		Entrance Island, 0.25 mi N of	49 12.80 123 48.40		
132		Departure Bay, entrance	49 12.40 123 55.85		
133		Whiskey-Golf, SE corner	49 14.83 123 48.40		

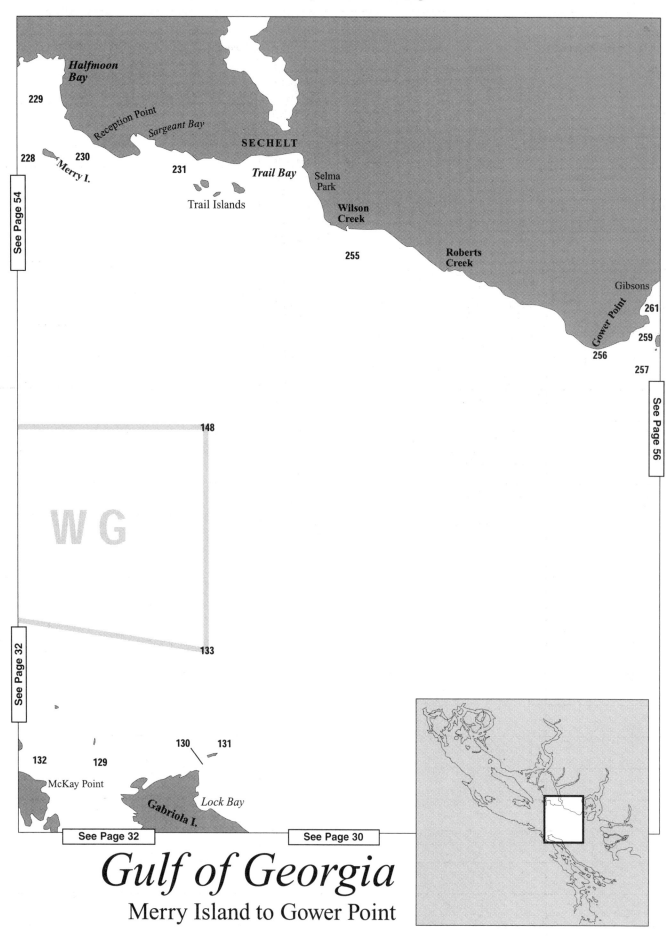

Halfmoon Bay

229

Reception Point

Sargeant Bay

SECHELT

228

230

Merry I.

231

Trail Bay

Selma Park

Trail Islands

Wilson Creek

255

Roberts Creek

Gibsons

Gower Point

261

259

256

257

See Page 54

See Page 56

148

W G

133

See Page 32

130 131

132 129

McKay Point

Lock Bay

Gabriola I.

See Page 32

See Page 30

Gulf of Georgia
Merry Island to Gower Point

Waypoint	Ship's Waypoint	Description	Latitude/ Longitude	TD1/ TD2 For Loran Only	Notes
129		Fairway Channel, middle, 0.3 mi S of Snake Island Reef light & bell buoy P2	49 12.20 123 53.15		
130		Forwood Channel, middle	49 12.25 123 49.00		
131		Entrance Island, 0.25 mi N of	49 12.80 123 48.40		
132		Departure Bay, entrance	49 12.40 123 55.85		
133		Whiskey-Golf, SE corner	49 14.83 123 48.40		
148		Whiskey-Golf, NE corner, off Halibut Bank	49 21.00 123 48.40		
228		Welcome Passage, S entrance, W of Merry Island	49 28.00 123 56.15		
229		Welcome Passage, middle (entrance to Halfmoon Bay)	49 29.50 123 55.90		
230		Welcome Passage, S entrance, E of Merry Island	49 28.00 123 53.80		
231		Passage between Trail Islands & Sechelt Peninsula, W entrance	49 27.70 123 49.80		
255		White Islets, 0.25 mi N of	49 25.50 123 42.70		
256		Gower Point, 0.25 mi S of	49 22.75 123 32.20		
257		Barfleur Passage, W entrance	49 22.30 123 30.45		
259		Shoal Channel, S entrance	49 23.10 123 30.40		
261		Gibsons, entrance	49 24.00 123 30.10		

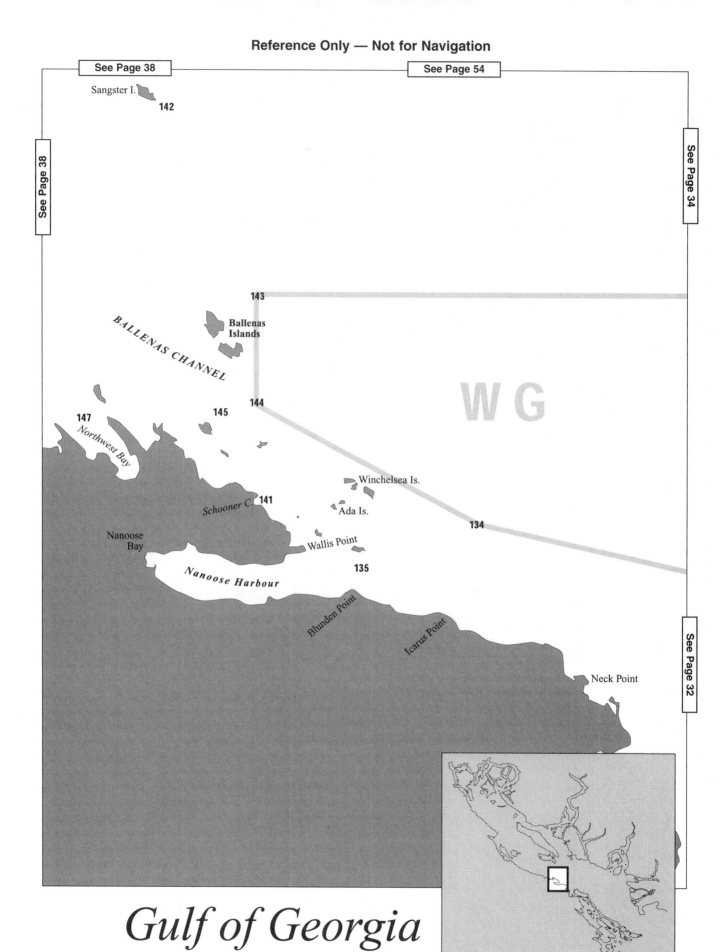

See Page 38
See Page 54
See Page 38
See Page 34
See Page 32

Sangster I.

142

BALLENAS CHANNEL

143

Ballenas Islands

W G

144

147

Northwest Bay

145

Winchelsea Is.

141

Schooner C.

Ada Is.

Nanoose
Bay

Wallis Point

134

135

Nanoose Harbour

Blunden Point

Icarus Point

Neck Point

Gulf of Georgia
Ballenas Channel and Nanoose Harbour

Waypoint	Ship's Waypoint	Description	Latitude/ Longitude	TD1/ TD2 *For Loran Only*	Notes
134		Whiskey-Golf, turn to clear Winchelsea Islands	49 16.75 124 00.90		
135		Nanoose Harbour, entrance, between Maude Island & Blunden Point	49 15.85 124 04.70		
141		Schooner Cove, entrance	49 17.30 124 07.90		
142		Sangster Island, Elephant Eye Point, 0.25 mi SE of	49 25.30 124 11.25		
143		Whiskey-Golf, NW corner, off Ballenas Islands	49 21.35 124 07.70		
144		Whiskey-Golf, SW corner, S of Ballenas Islands	49 19.35 124 07.70		
145		Gerald Island, 0.25 mi NNE of	49 19.00 124 09.45		
147		Northwest Bay, entrance	49 18.90 124 13.40		

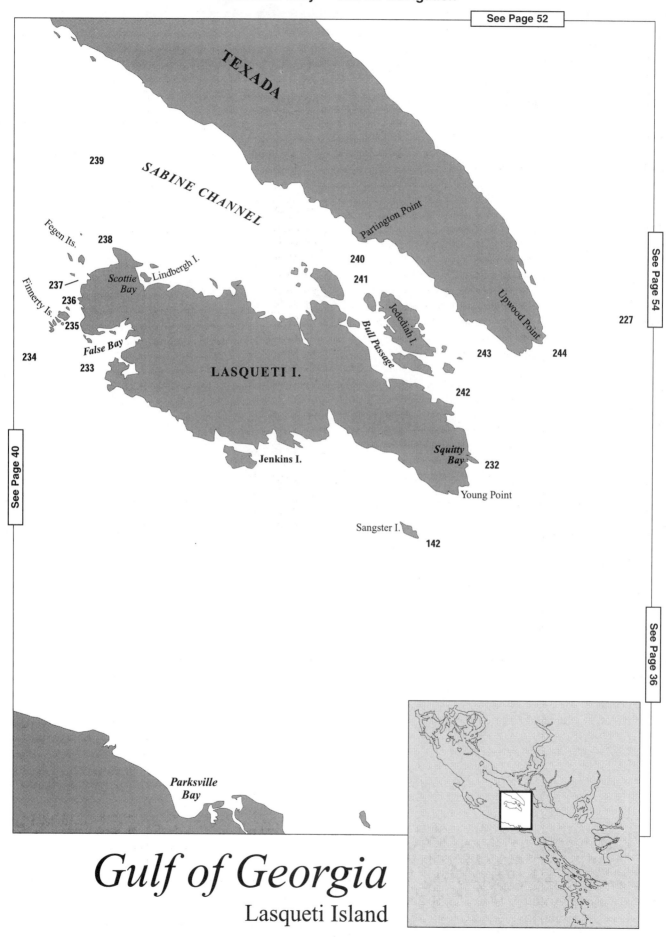

See Page 52

See Page 54

See Page 40

See Page 36

TEXADA

SABINE CHANNEL

239

Fegen Its.

238

Partington Point

240

241

Upwood Point

237

Scottie Bay

Lindbergh I.

Finnerty Is.

236

Jedediah I.

235

Bull Passage

243

244

227

234

False Bay

233

LASQUETI I.

242

Squitty Bay

232

Jenkins I.

Young Point

Sangster I.

142

Gulf of Georgia
Lasqueti Island

Parksville Bay

Waypoint	Ship's Waypoint	Description	Latitude/ Longitude	TD1/ TD2 *For Loran Only*	Notes
142		Sangster Island, Elephant Eye Point, 0.25 mi SE of	49 25.30 124 11.25		
227		Malaspina Strait, S entrance	49 30.00 124 04.95		
232		Squitty Bay, entrance, 0.25 mi S of	49 27.00 124 09.40		
233		False Bay, entrance	49 29.05 124 22.70		
234		Stevens Passage, middle, E of Sisters Islets	49 29.30 124 24.80		
235		Passage between Finnerty Islands & Lasqueti Island, S entrance	49 29.90 124 23.10		
236		Passage between Finnerty Islands & Lasqueti Island, N entrance	49 30.40 124 23.10		
237		Passage between Fegen (Fegan) Islets & Lasqueti Island, S entrance	49 30.85 124 33.05		
238		Passage between Fegen (Fegan) Islets & Lasqueti Island, N entrance	49 31.70 124 22.15		
239		Sabine Channel, W entrance	49 33.40 124 22.55		
240		Sabine Channel, between Jervis Island & Partington Point	49 31.30 124 13.75		
241		Bull Passage, N entrance, E of Jervis Island	49 30.90 124 13.70		
242		Bull Passage, SE entrance	49 28.50 124 10.20		
243		Sabine Channel, E entrance	49 29.30 124 09.55		
244		Upwood Point, 0.25 mi SE of	49 29.25 124 07.20		

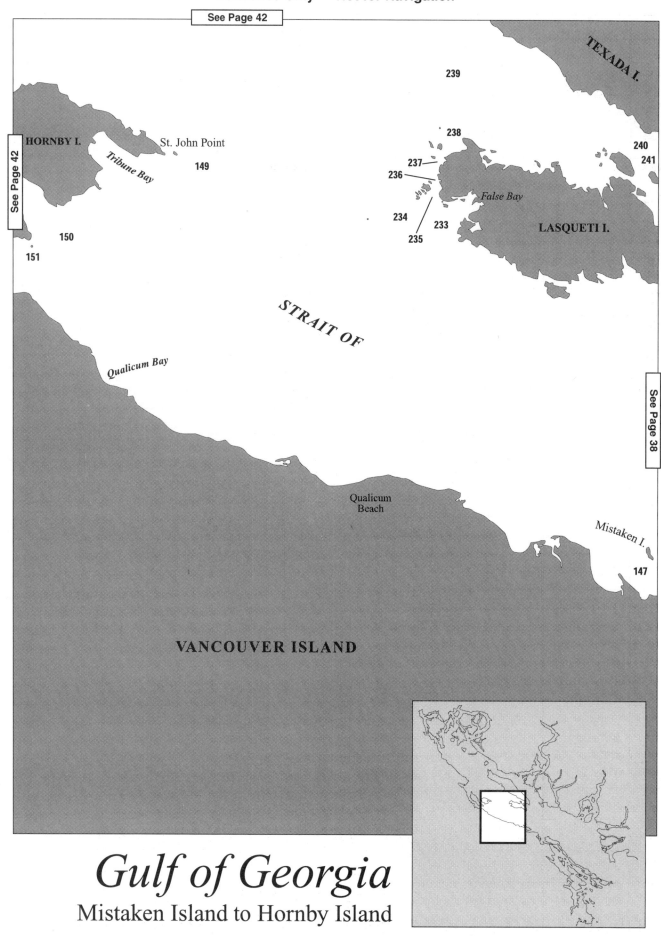

See Page 42

TEXADA I.

239

238

237

236

240
241

234
235

233

False Bay

LASQUETI I.

See Page 42

HORNBY I.

St. John Point

Tribune Bay

149

150

151

STRAIT OF

Qualicum Bay

See Page 38

Qualicum
Beach

Mistaken I.

147

VANCOUVER ISLAND

Gulf of Georgia
Mistaken Island to Hornby Island

Waypoint	Ship's Waypoint	Description	Latitude/ Longitude	TD1/ TD2 *For Loran Only*	Notes
147		Northwest Bay, entrance	49 18.90 124 13.40		
149		Hornby Island, 1 mi SE of St. John Point	49 30.60 124 33.65		
150		Lambert Channel, S entrance	49 28.55 124 39.75		
151		Baynes Sound, entrance, mid-channel	49 28.00 124 41.30		
233		False Bay, entrance	49 29.05 124 22.70		
234		Stevens Passage, middle, E of Sisters Islets	49 29.30 124 24.80		
235		Passage between Finnerty Islands & Lasqueti Island, S entrance	49 29.90 124 23.10		
236		Passage between Finnerty Islands & Lasqueti Island, N entrance	49 30.40 124 23.10		
237		Passage between Fegen (Fegan) Islets & Lasqueti Island, S entrance	49 30.85 124 33.05		
238		Passage between Fegen (Fegan) Islets & Lasqueti Island, N entrance	49 31.70 124 22.15		
239		Sabine Channel, W entrance	49 33.40 124 22.55		
240		Sabine Channel, between Jervis Island & Partington Point	49 31.30 124 13.75		
241		Bull Passage, N entrance, E of Jervis Island	49 30.90 124 13.70		

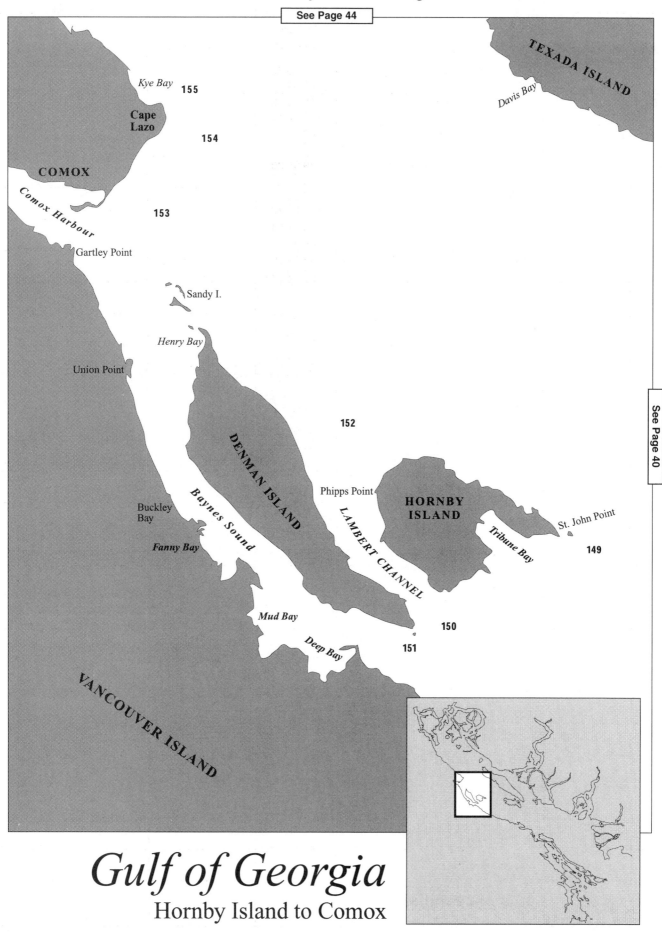

See Page 44

TEXADA ISLAND

Kye Bay 155

Davis Bay

Cape
Lazo

154

COMOX

153

Comox Harbour

Gartley Point

Sandy I.

Henry Bay

Union Point

152

See Page 40

DENMAN ISLAND

Phipps Point

HORNBY
ISLAND

St. John Point

Buckley
Bay

Baynes Sound

LAMBERT CHANNEL

Tribune Bay

149

Fanny Bay

Mud Bay

150

Deep Bay

151

VANCOUVER ISLAND

Gulf of Georgia
Hornby Island to Comox

Waypoint	Ship's Waypoint	Description	Latitude/ Longitude	TD1/ TD2 *For Loran Only*	Notes
149		Hornby Island, 1 mi SE of St. John Point	49 30.60 124 33.65		
150		Lambert Channel, S entrance	49 28.55 124 39.75		
151		Baynes Sound, entrance, mid-channel	49 28.00 124 41.30		
152		Lambert Channel, N entrance	49 34.00 124 43.90		
153		Comox Bar light and bell buoy P54	49 39.50 124 51.70		
154		East Cardinal buoy PJ, 1.5 mi SE of Cape Lazo	49 41.50 124 49.70		
155		East Cardinal buoy PK, 0.25 mi NE of	49 42.80 124 50.60		

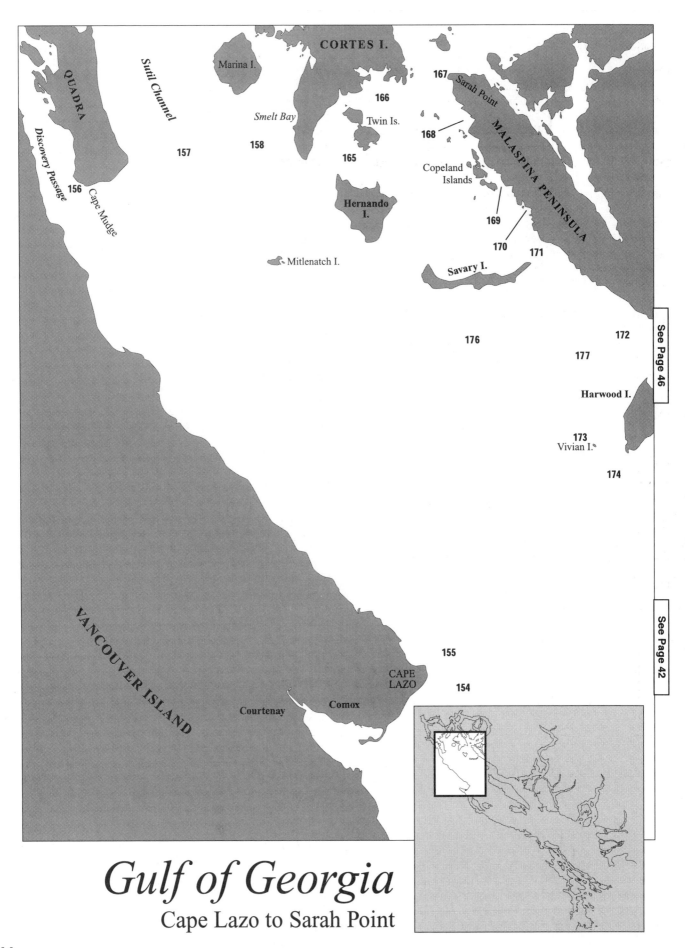

CORTES I.

Marina I.

QUADRA

Sutil Channel

Discovery Passage

Cape Mudge

Smelt Bay

Twin Is.

167

Sarah Point

MALASPINA PENINSULA

166

168

Copeland Islands

169

170 171

157

158

165

Hernando I.

Mitlenatch I.

Savary I.

176

172

177

Harwood I.

See Page 46

173

Vivian I.

174

155

CAPE LAZO

154

VANCOUVER ISLAND

Courtenay

Comox

See Page 42

Gulf of Georgia
Cape Lazo to Sarah Point

Waypoint	Ship's Waypoint	Description	Latitude/ Longitude	TD1/ TD2 For Loran Only	Notes
154		East Cardinal buoy PJ, 1.5 mi SE of Cape Lazo	49 41.50 124 49.70		
155		East Cardinal buoy PK, 0.25 mi NE of	49 42.80 124 50.60		
156		Discovery Passage, entrance, S of Cape Mudge Sector light	49 59.75 125 11.90		
157		Sutil Channel, S entrance, middle	50 01.00 125 06.00		
158		Sutil Channel, E side (approach to Manson Bay/Gorge Harbour)	50 01.30 125 02.00		
165		Baker Passage, middle, between Twin Islands & Spilsbury Point	50 00.70 124 56.30		
166		Approach to Cortes Bay, between Three Islets & Twin Islands	50 02.70 124 55.00		
167		Sarah Point, 0.25 mi W of	50 03.80 124 51.00		
168		Thulin Passage, NW entrance	50 02.00 124 49.60		
169		Thulin Passage, SE entrance	49 59.65 124 47.45		
170		Lund, entrance, middle	49 58.85 124 46.15		
171		Savary Island, E of, mid-channel between Mace Point and Hurtado Point	49 57.40 124 45.40		
172		Shearwater Passage, N entrance	49 54.30 124 40.70		
173		Shearwater Passage, S entrance, 0.5 mi W of Vivian Island	49 50.70 124 42.95		
174		Algerine Passage, W entrance	49 49.30 124 41.25		
176		Savary Island, S of, between Stradiotti Reef & Grant Reefs	49 54.30 124 50.15		
177		Mystery Reef, 0.7 mi S of	49 53.65 124 42.85		

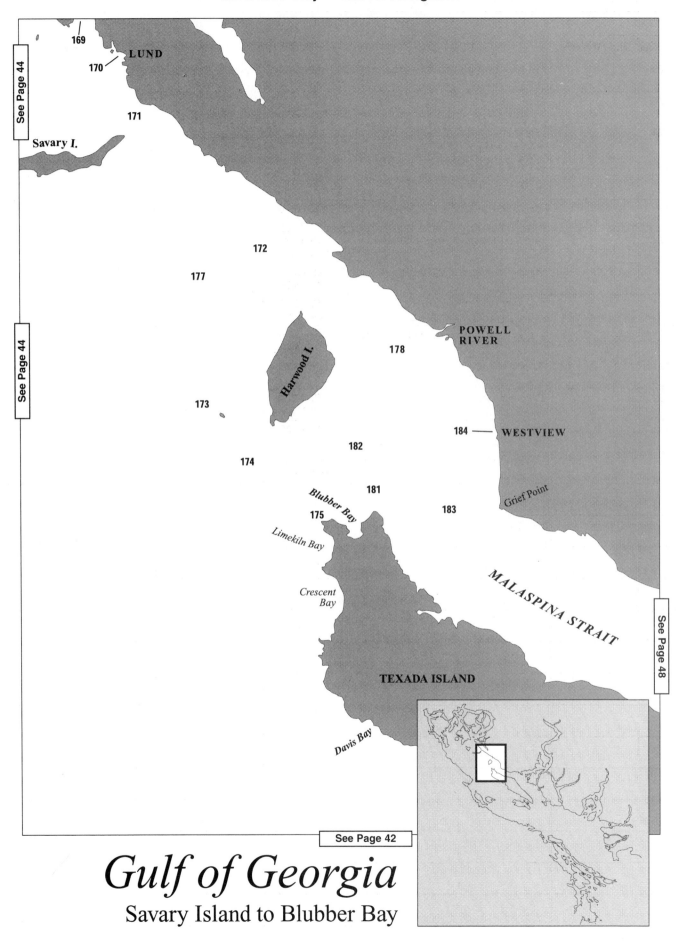

169

LUND

170

171

Savary I.

See Page 44

See Page 44

172

177

POWELL
RIVER

Harwood I.

178

173

184 — WESTVIEW

182

174

Grief Point

181

Blubber Bay

183

175

Limekiln Bay

MALASPINA STRAIT

Crescent
Bay

See Page 48

TEXADA ISLAND

Davis Bay

See Page 42

Gulf of Georgia
Savary Island to Blubber Bay

Waypoint	Ship's Waypoint	Description	Latitude/ Longitude	TD1/ TD2 *For Loran Only*	Notes
169		Thulin Passage, SE entrance	49 59.65 124 47.45		
170		Lund, entrance, middle	49 58.85 124 46.15		
171		Savary Island, E of, mid-channel between Mace Point and Hurtado Point	49 57.40 124 45.40		
172		Shearwater Passage, N entrance	49 54.30 124 40.70		
173		Shearwater Passage, S entrance, 0.5 mi W of Vivian Island	49 50.70 124 42.95		
174		Algerine Passage, W entrance	49 49.30 124 41.25		
175		Kiddie Point, 0.25 mi NW of	49 48.10 124 38.60		
177		Mystery Reef, 0.7 mi S of	49 53.65 124 42.85		
178		Harwood Island, E of, mid-channel	49 52.05 124 35.45		
181		Grilse Point, 0.5 mi N of	49 48.70 124 36.45		
182		Algerine Passage, E entrance	49 49.70 124 37.20		
183		Malaspina Strait, N entrance, between Grilse Point & Grief Point	49 48.20 124 33.70		
184		Westview Boat Harbour, S entrance	49 49.95 124 32.10		

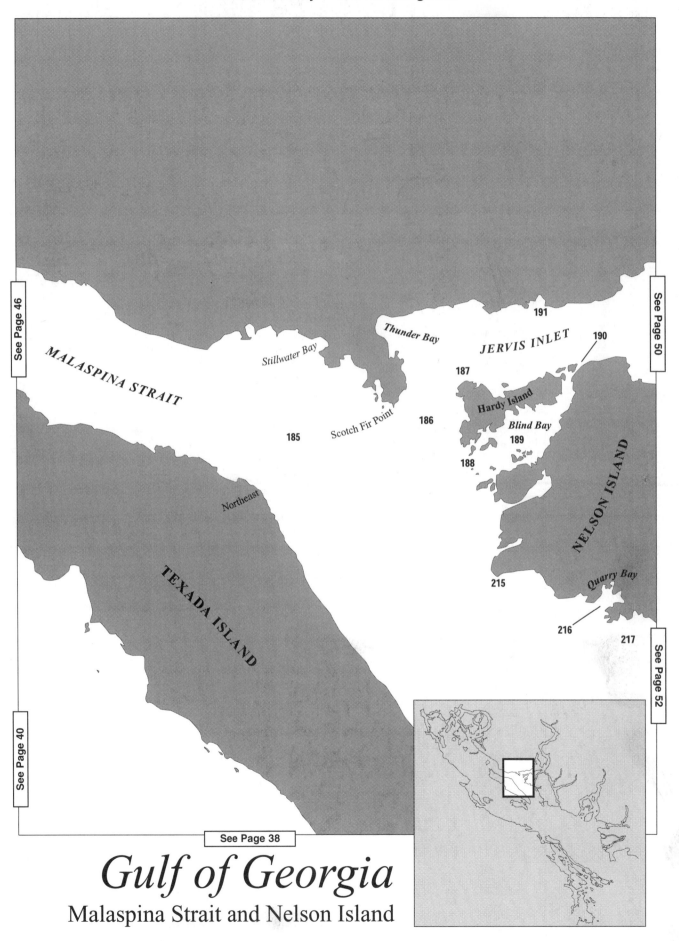

See Page 46

See Page 50

See Page 52

See Page 40

See Page 38

MALASPINA STRAIT

Stillwater Bay

Thunder Bay

JERVIS INLET

191

190

187

Hardy Island

Blind Bay

189

Scotch Fir Point

186

185

188

NELSON ISLAND

Northeast

TEXADA ISLAND

215

Quarry Bay

216

217

Gulf of Georgia
Malaspina Strait and Nelson Island

48

Waypoint	Ship's Waypoint	Description	Latitude/ Longitude	TD1/ TD2 For Loran Only	Notes
185		Malaspina Strait, middle, NE of Northeast Point	49 43.70 124 20.20		
186		Jervis Inlet, entrance	49 44.10 124 14.85		
187		Jervis Inlet, 0.25 mi NW of Ball Point	49 45.30 124 13.60		
188		Blind Bay, entrance	49 43.00 124 13.35		
189		Blind Bay, middle	49 43.60 124 11.45		
190		Jervis Inlet, entrance to Telescope Passage	49 45.60 124 08.80		
191		Jervis Inlet, entrance to Saltery Bay	49 46.60 124 10.50		
215		Cape Cockburn, 0.25 mi S of	49 40.10 124 12.40		
216		Quarry Bay, entrance	49 39.40 124 08.30		
217		Nelson Rock light	49 38.65 124 07.25		

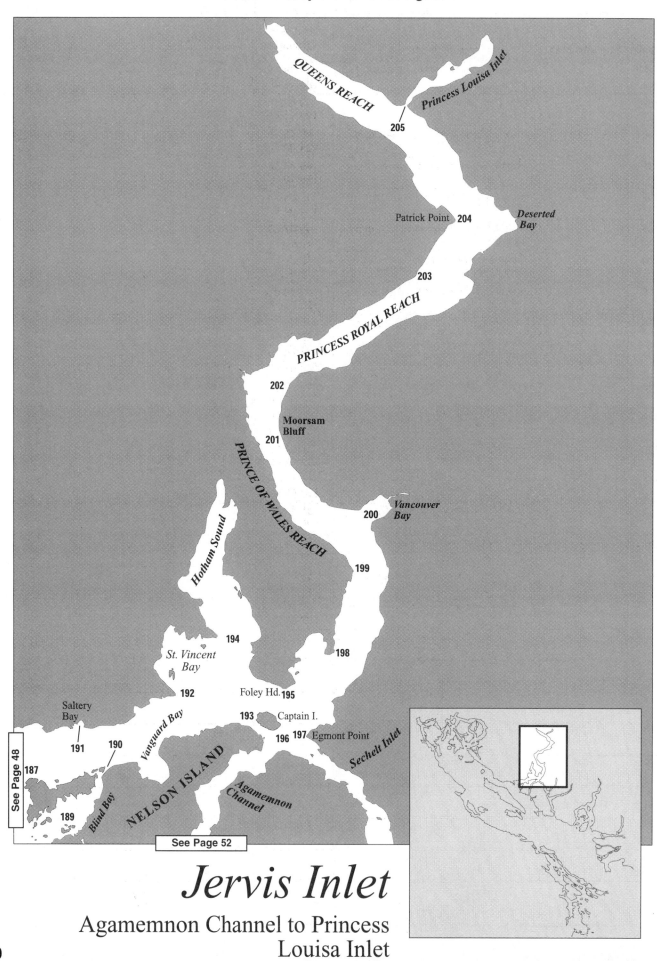

QUEENS REACH

Princess Louisa Inlet

205

Patrick Point 204

Deserted Bay

203

PRINCESS ROYAL REACH

202

Moorsam Bluff

201

PRINCE OF WALES REACH

Vancouver Bay

200

199

Hotham Sound

194

St. Vincent Bay

198

192

Foley Hd. 195

Saltery Bay

193 Captain I.

196 197 Egmont Point

Vanguard Bay

Sechelt Inlet

191 190

187

189 Blind Bay

NELSON ISLAND

Agamemnon Channel

See Page 48

See Page 52

Jervis Inlet

Agamemnon Channel to Princess Louisa Inlet

Waypoint	Ship's Waypoint	Description	Latitude/ Longitude	TD1/ TD2 *For Loran Only*	Notes
187		Jervis Inlet, 0.25 mi NW of Ball Point	49 45.30 124 13.60		
189		Blind Bay, middle	49 43.60 124 11.45		
190		Jervis Inlet, entrance to Telescope Passage	49 45.60 124 08.80		
191		Jervis Inlet, entrance to Saltery Bay	49 46.60 124 10.50		
192		Jervis Inlet, Culloden Point, 0.25 mi E of	49 48.00 124 04.35		
193		Jervis Inlet, NW entrance to Agnew Passage	49 47.20 124 00.60		
194		Hotham Sound, entrance, E of Elephant Point	49 50.00 124 01.65		
195		Jervis Inlet, Foley Head, 0.25 mi S of	49 48.00 123 58.15		
196		Agamemnon Channel, N entrance	49 46.30 123 58.65		
197		Egmont Point, 0.25 mi W of	49 46.50 123 57.20		
198		Jervis Inlet, Dacres Point, 0.25 mi E of	49 49.60 123 55.00		
199		Jervis Inlet, Saumarez Bluff, 0.25 mi E of	49 52.70 123 53.85		
200		Vancouver Bay, entrance	49 54.65 123 53.50		
201		Jervis Inlet, Marlborough Heights, 0.25 mi SW of Moorsam Bluff	49 57.30 123 58.80		
202		Jervis Inlet, SE entrance to Princess Royal Reach	49 59.40 123 59.00		
203		Jervis Inlet, Princess Royal Reach, 0.25 mi off W side	50 03.30 123 50.15		
204		Jervis Inlet, Patrick Point, 0.25 mi E of	50 05.50 123 47.65		
205		Jervis Inlet, Malibu Rapids, entrance	50 09.65 123 51.25		

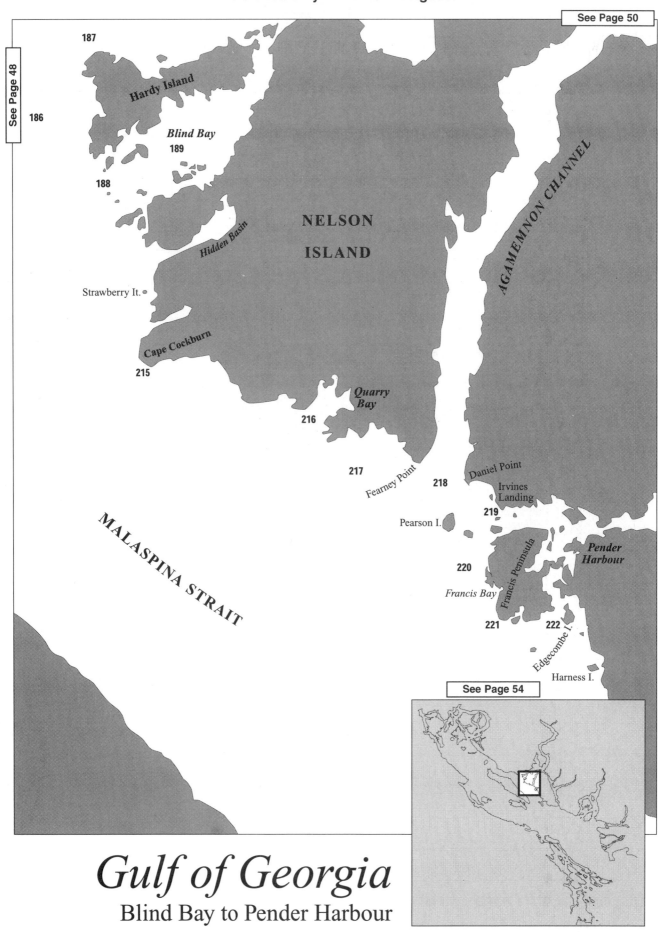

See Page 50
See Page 48
See Page 54

187

186

Hardy Island

Blind Bay
189

188

Hidden Basin

NELSON ISLAND

Strawberry It.

Cape Cockburn

215

Quarry Bay

216

217

Fearney Point

218

Daniel Point

Irvines Landing

219

Pearson I.

AGAMEMNON CHANNEL

Pender Harbour

220

Francis Peninsula

Francis Bay

221

222

Edgecombe I.

Harness I.

MALASPINA STRAIT

Gulf of Georgia
Blind Bay to Pender Harbour

Waypoint	Ship's Waypoint	Description	Latitude/ Longitude	TD1/ TD2 *For Loran Only*	Notes
186		Jervis Inlet, entrance	49 44.10 124 14.85		
187		Jervis Inlet, 0.25 mi NW of Ball Point	49 45.30 124 13.60		
188		Blind Bay, entrance	49 43.00 124 13.35		
189		Blind Bay, middle	49 43.60 124 11.45		
215		Cape Cockburn, 0.25 mi S of	49 40.10 124 12.40		
216		Quarry Bay, entrance	49 39.40 124 08.30		
217		Nelson Rock light	49 38.65 124 07.25		
218		Agamemnon Channel, S entrance	49 38.35 124 05.10		
219		Pender Harbour, entrance, between Henry Point & Williams Island	49 37.85 124 03.75		
220		Pender Harbour, S approach, off Francis Peninsula	49 37.00 124 04.45		
221		Francis Point, 0.25 mi SW of	49 36.05 124 03.90		
222		Bargain Bay, entrance	49 36.15 124 02.25		

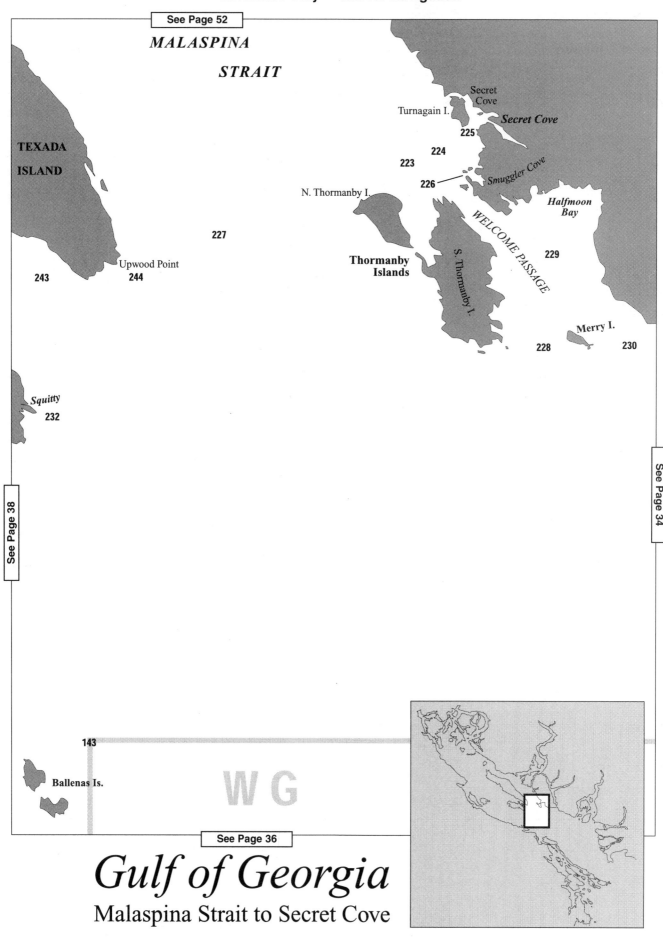

See Page 52

MALASPINA

STRAIT

Secret
Cove

Turnagain I.

Secret Cove

225

224

223

226

Smuggler Cove

N. Thormanby I.

*Halfmoon
Bay*

TEXADA

ISLAND

227

WELCOME PASSAGE

229

**Thormanby
Islands**

S. Thormanby I.

Upwood Point

243   **244**

Merry I.

228   **230**

See Page 38

Squitty

232

See Page 34

143

Ballenas Is.

W G

See Page 36

Gulf of Georgia

Malaspina Strait to Secret Cove

Waypoint	Ship's Waypoint	Description	Latitude/ Longitude	TD1/ TD2 *For Loran Only*	Notes
143		Whiskey-Golf, NW corner, off Ballenas Islands	49 21.35 124 07.70		
223		Buccaneer Bay, entrance	49 31.10 123 59.85		
224		Welcome Passage, N entrance	49 31.30 123 58.95		
225		Secret Cove, entrance	49 31.65 123 58.10		
226		Smuggler Cove, entrance	49 30.90 123 58.25		
227		Malaspina Strait, S entrance	49 30.00 124 04.95		
228		Welcome Passage, S entrance, W of Merry Island	49 28.00 123 56.15		
229		Welcome Passage, middle (entrance to Halfmoon Bay)	49 29.50 123 55.90		
230		Welcome Passage, S entrance, E of Merry Island	49 28.00 123 53.80		
232		Squitty Bay, entrance, 0.25 mi S of	49 27.00 124 09.40		
243		Sabine Channel, E entrance	49 29.30 124 09.55		
244		Upwood Point, 0.25 mi SE of	49 29.25 124 07.20		

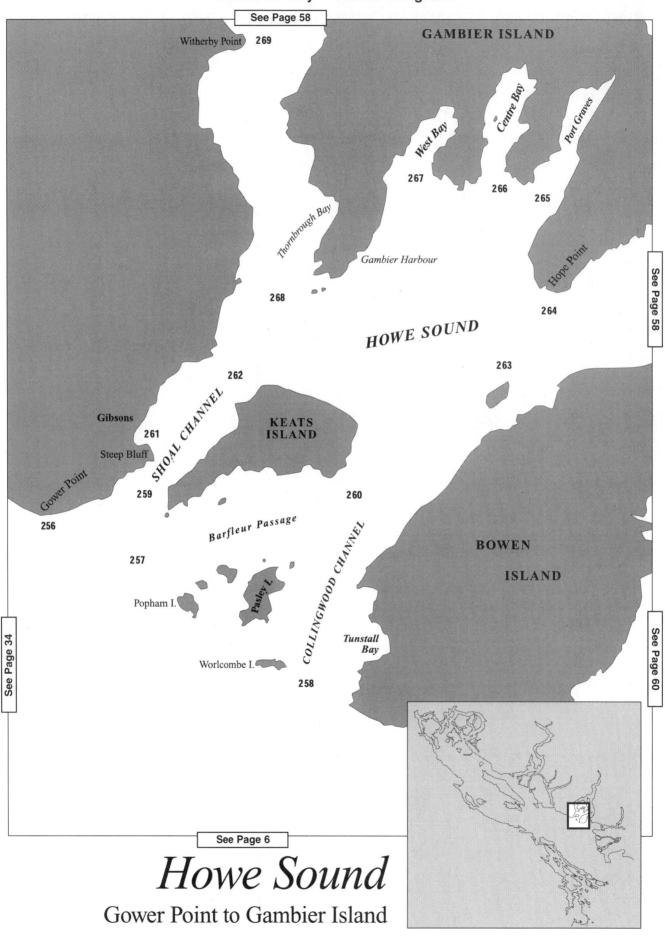

Reference Only — Not for Navigation

Howe Sound

Gower Point to Gambier Island

Waypoint	Ship's Waypoint	Description	Latitude/ Longitude	TD1/ TD2 For Loran Only	Notes
256		Gower Point, 0.25 mi S of	49 22.75 123 32.20		
257		Barfleur Passage, W entrance	49 22.30 123 30.45		
258		Collingwood Channel, S entrance	49 20.60 123 26.90		
259		Shoal Channel, S entrance	49 23.10 123 30.40		
260		Barfleur Passage/Collingwood Channel, N entrances	49 23.20 123 25.95		
261		Gibsons, entrance	49 24.00 123 30.10		
262		Shoal Channel, N entrance	49 24.75 123 28.55		
263		Hutt Island, 0.25 mi N of	49 24.95 123 22.95		
264		Hope Point, 0.25 mi S of	49 25.60 123 22.15		
265		Gambier Island, Port Graves, entrance	49 27.10 123 22.30		
266		Gambier Island, Centre Bay, entrance	49 27.20 123 23.20		
267		Gambier Island, West Bay, entrance	49 27.40 123 24.85		
268		Thornbrough Channel, S entrance	49 25.65 123 27.55		
269		Thornbrough Channel, 0.25 mi E of Witherby Point	49 29.15 123 27.95		

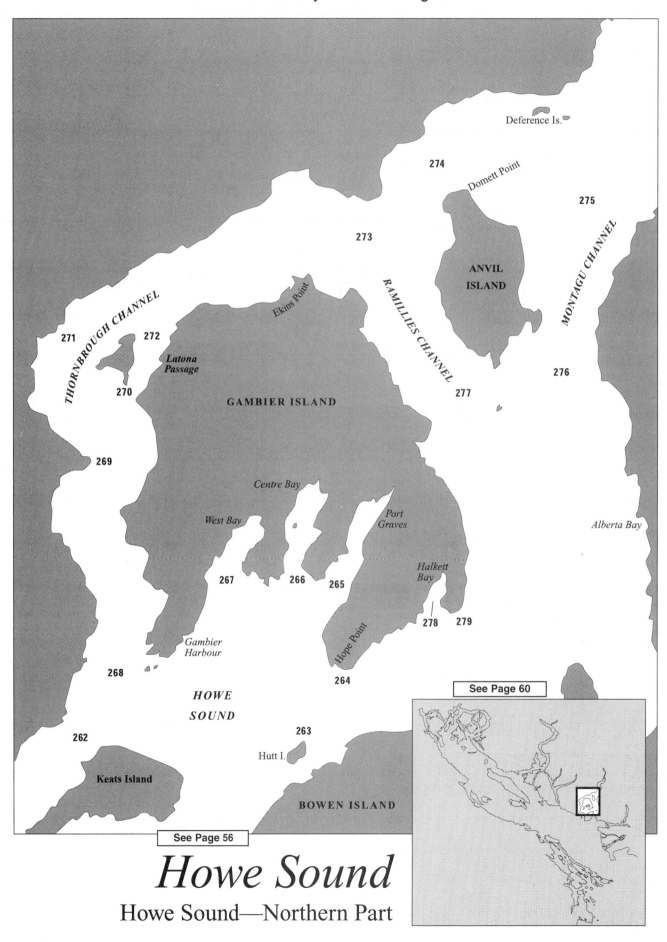

Deference Is.

274

Domett Point

275

273

ANVIL ISLAND

THORNBROUGH CHANNEL

RAMILLIES CHANNEL

MONTAGU CHANNEL

Ekins Point

271 272

Latona Passage

270

276

GAMBIER ISLAND

277

269

Centre Bay

West Bay

Port Graves

Alberta Bay

267 266 265

Halkett Bay

Hope Point

278 279

Gambier Harbour

268

HOWE SOUND

264

262

263

Hutt I.

Keats Island

BOWEN ISLAND

See Page 60

See Page 56

Howe Sound

Howe Sound—Northern Part

Waypoint	Ship's Waypoint	Description	Latitude/ Longitude	TD1/ TD2 For Loran Only	Notes
262		Shoal Channel, N entrance	49 24.75 123 28.55		
263		Hutt Island, 0.25 mi N of	49 24.95 123 22.95		
264		Hope Point, 0.25 mi S of	49 25.60 123 22.15		
265		Gambier Island, Port Graves, entrance	49 27.10 123 22.30		
266		Gambier Island, Centre Bay, entrance	49 27.20 123 23.20		
267		Gambier Island, West Bay, entrance	49 27.40 123 24.85		
268		Thornbrough Channel, S entrance	49 25.65 123 27.55		
269		Thornbrough Channel, 0.25 mi E of Witherby Point	49 29.15 123 27.95		
270		Latona Passage, S entrance	49 30.20 123 27.30		
271		Thornbrough Channel, 0.25 mi SE of Port Mellon	49 31.00 123 28.90		
272		Latona Passage, N entrance	49 31.15 123 26.70		
273		Ramillies Channel, N entrance	49 32.60 123 21.35		
274		Anvil Island, 0.4 mi N of Domett Point	49 33.80 123 19.65		
275		Montagu Channel, N entrance	49 33.50 123 16.25		
276		Montagu Channel, S entrance	49 30.55 123 16.60		
277		Ramillies Channel, S entrance	49 30.20 123 19.30		
278		Halkett Bay, entrance	49 26.80 123 19.80		
279		Halkett Point, 0.25 mi SE of	49 26.60 123 19.00		

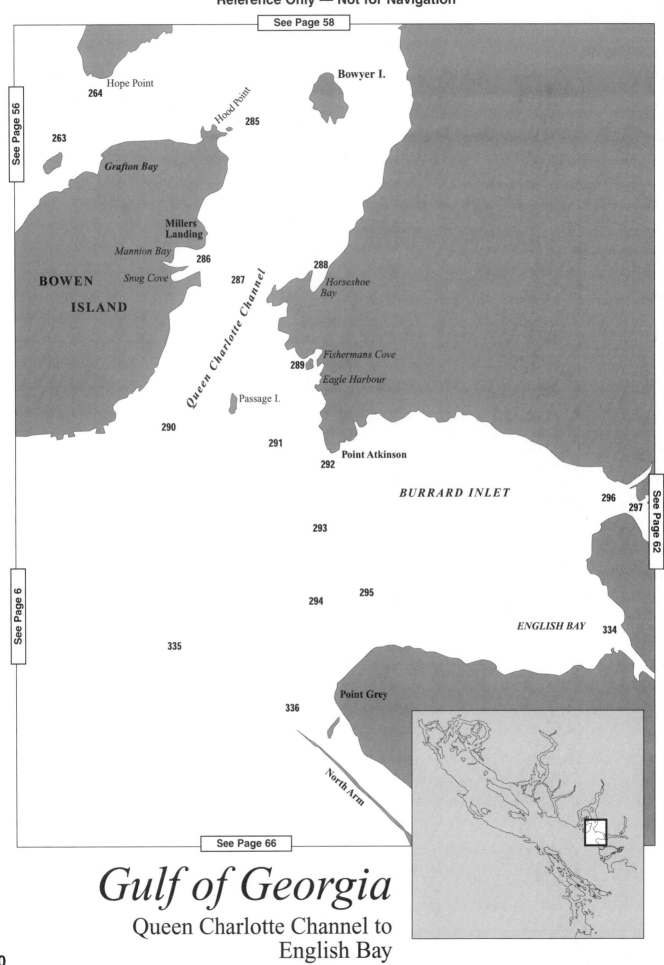

See Page 58

Bowyer I.

Hope Point
264

See Page 56

Hood Point
285

263

Grafton Bay

Millers Landing

Mannion Bay
286

288

Horseshoe Bay

BOWEN

Snug Cove
287

Queen Charlotte Channel

ISLAND

Fishermans Cove

289

Eagle Harbour

Passage I.

290

291

Point Atkinson
292

BURRARD INLET

296

297

See Page 62

293

See Page 6

295

294

ENGLISH BAY
334

335

Point Grey

336

North Arm

See Page 66

Gulf of Georgia
Queen Charlotte Channel to
English Bay

Waypoint	Ship's Waypoint	Description	Latitude/ Longitude	TD1/ TD2 *For Loran Only*	Notes
263		Hutt Island, 0.25 mi N of	49 24.95 123 22.95		
264		Hope Point, 0.25 mi S of	49 25.60 123 22.15		
285		Finisterre Island, 0.25 mi ENE of	49 25.15 123 18.15		
286		Mannion Bay, entrance	49 23.00 123 19.30		
287		Queen Charlotte Channel, between Lookout Point & Bowen Island	49 22.65 123 18.35		
288		Horseshoe Bay, entrance	49 22.95 123 16.25		
289		Fishermans Cove, entrance	49 21.15 123 16.85		
290		Queen Charlotte Channel, entrance, between Point Cowan & Passage Island	49 20.20 123 20.25		
291		Queen Charlotte Channel, S entrance, between Passage Island & Point Atkinson	49 20.00 123 17.50		
292		Point Atkinson, 0.25 mi S of	49 19.60 123 16.00		
293		Burrard Inlet, entrance	49 18.40 123 16.10		
294		Point Grey light and bell buoy Q62	49 17.35 123 16.00		
295		Spanish Bank, 0.25 mi N of	49 17.60 123 15.10		
296		First Narrows, W entrance	49 19.05 123 09.00		
297		Lions Gate Bridge, mid-span	49 18.90 123 08.30		
334		False Creek, entrance	49 17.00 123 09.00		
335		Vancouver Approach Cautionary light buoy QA	49 16.60 123 19.30		
336		North Arm Fraser River, entrance	49 15.70 123 18.05		

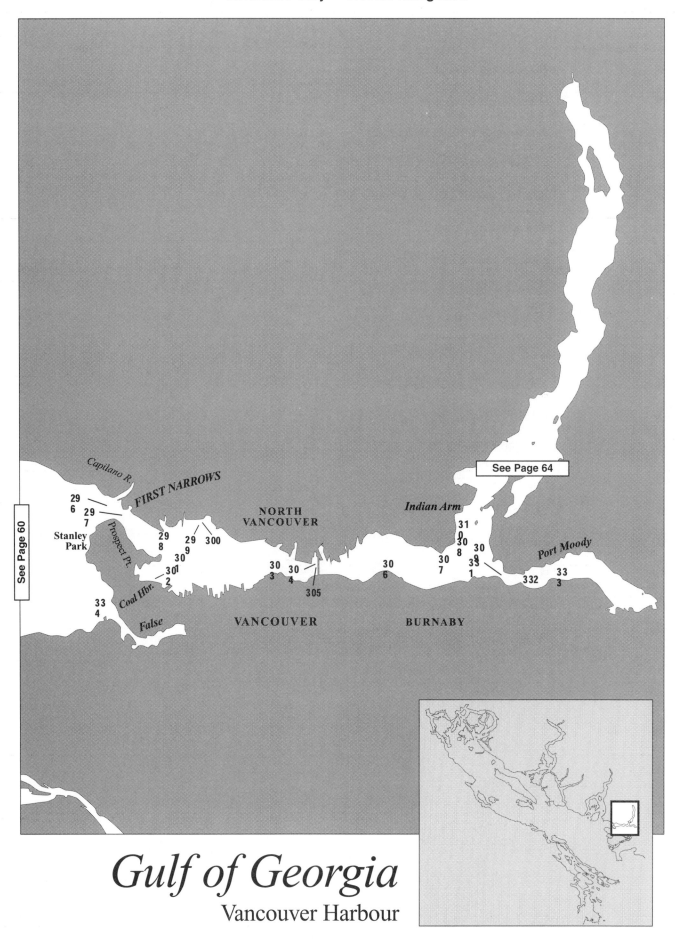

See Page 64

See Page 60

Capilano R.

FIRST NARROWS

NORTH
VANCOUVER

Indian Arm

Port Moody

Stanley
Park

Prospect Pt.

29
6
29
7

29
8

29
9

300

31
0

30
8

30
9
33
1

30
7

332

33
3

30
9

30
3

30
1
2

Coal Hbr.

False

30
3

30
4

305

30
6

30
7

VANCOUVER

BURNABY

33
4

Gulf of Georgia

Vancouver Harbour

Waypoint	Ship's Waypoint	Description	Latitude/ Longitude	TD1/ TD2 For Loran Only	Notes
296		First Narrows, W entrance	49 19.05 123 09.00		
297		Lions Gate Bridge, mid-span	49 18.90 123 08.30		
298		Vancouver Harbour, S of Vancouver wharves	49 18.45 123 06.85		
299		Vancouver Harbour, off Burrard Yacht Club breakwater	49 18.60 123 05.65		
300		Vancouver Harbour, Mosquito Creek Marina, entrance	49 18.65 123 05.45		
301		Vancouver Harbour, Burnaby Shoal, E of	49 17.90 123 06.50		
302		Vancouver Harbour, Coal Harbour entrance	49 17.50 123 07.20		
303		Vancouver Harbour, W approach to Second Narrows Bridge	49 17.75 123 03.05		
304		Vancouver Harbour, Lynnwood Marina, entrance	49 17.80 123 01.70		
305		Vancouver Harbour, Second Narrows Bridge, center	49 17.70 123 01.60		
306		Vancouver Harbour, 0.25 mi N of Berry Point	49 17.95 122 59.25		
307		Vancouver Harbour, 0.25 mi S of Roche Point	49 17.75 122 57.35		
308		Indian Arm, entrance, W side	49 18.25 122 56.55		
309		Indian Arm, entrance, E side	49 18.20 122 56.05		
310		Indian Arm, W of Boulder Island	49 18.70 122 56.45		
331		Port Moody, entrance	49 17.60 122 55.35		
332		Port Moody, S of Carraholly	49 17.50 122 54.55		
333		Reed Point Marina, W entrance	49 17.60 122 53.30		
334		False Creek, entrance	49 17.00 123 09.00		

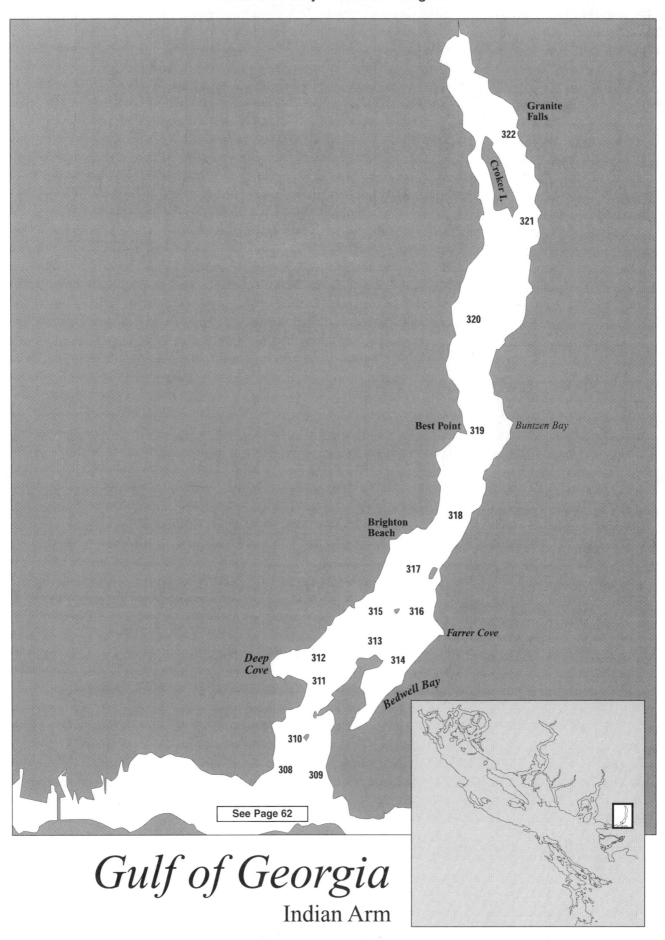

Granite
Falls

322

Croker I.

321

320

Best Point 319 *Buntzen Bay*

318

Brighton
Beach

317

315 316

Farrer Cove

313

Deep
Cove 312

314

311

Bedwell Bay

310

308 309

See Page 62

Gulf of Georgia
Indian Arm

Waypoint	Ship's Waypoint	Description	Latitude/ Longitude	TD1/ TD2 *For Loran Only*	Notes
308		Indian Arm, entrance, W side	49 18.25 122 56.55		
309		Indian Arm, entrance, E side	49 18.20 122 56.05		
310		Indian Arm, W of Boulder Island	49 18.70 122 56.45		
311		Indian Arm, entrance to Deep Cove, S side	49 19.55 122 56.00		
312		Indian Arm, entrance to Deep Cove, N side	49 19.85 122 56.00		
313		Indian Arm, N of Jug Island	49 19.95 122 54.85		
314		Indian Arm, Bedwell Bay, entrance	49 19.75 122 54.25		
315		Indian Arm, between Racoon Island & Lone Rock Point	49 20.45 122 54.75		
316		Indian Arm, E of Racoon Island	49 20.45 122 53.95		
317		Indian Arm, W of Twin Islands	49 21.05 122 53.95		
318		Indian Arm, mid-channel	49 21.80 122 53.05		
319		Indian Arm, E of Best Point	49 22.85 122 52.60		
320		Indian Arm, E of Silver Falls	49 24.45 122 52.70		
321		Indian Arm, SE of Croker Island	49 25.75 122 51.65		
322		Indian Arm, S of Granite Falls	49 26.90 122 51.85		

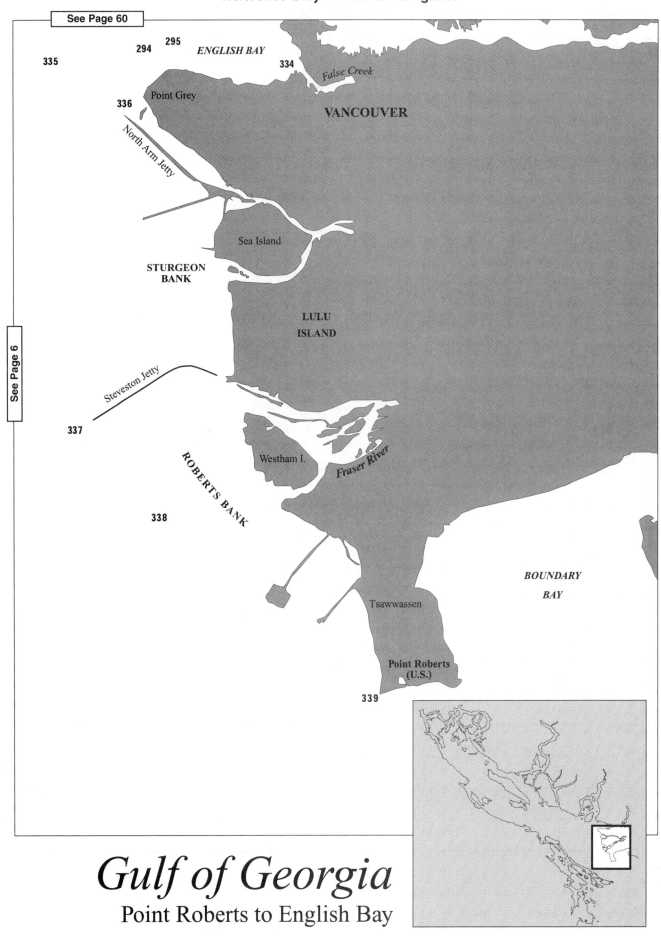

See Page 60

335

294 295 *ENGLISH BAY* 334

False Creek

Point Grey 336

VANCOUVER

North Arm Jetty

Sea Island

STURGEON BANK

See Page 6

LULU ISLAND

Steveston Jetty

337

ROBERT'S BANK

Westham I.

Fraser River

338

BOUNDARY BAY

Tsawwassen

Point Roberts (U.S.)

339

Gulf of Georgia
Point Roberts to English Bay

Waypoint	Ship's Waypoint	Description	Latitude/ Longitude	TD1/ TD2 *For Loran Only*	Notes
294		Point Grey light and bell buoy Q62	49 17.35 123 16.00		
295		Spanish Bank, 0.25 mi N of	49 17.60 123 15.10		
334		False Creek, entrance	49 17.00 123 09.00		
335		Vancouver Approach Cautionary light buoy QA	49 16.60 123 19.30		
336		North Arm Fraser River, entrance	49 15.70 123 18.05		
337		Steveston Jetty, entrance	49 05.90 123 19.20		
338		Canoe Pass light and bell buoy T14	49 02.30 123 15.40		
339		Point Roberts, 0.25 mi S of	48 58.00 123 05.30		

Index

W

Z

Notes

Notes

Notes

Notes

Ship's Waypoint Log

Waypoint No.	Description	Latitude/ Longitude

Ship's Waypoint Log

Waypoint No.	Description	Latitude/ Longitude

Ship's Waypoint Log

Waypoint No.	Description	Latitude/ Longitude

Ship's Waypoint Log

Waypoint No.	Description	Latitude/ Longitude

Ship's Waypoint Log

Waypoint No.	Description	Latitude/ Longitude